Royal Society of Medicine

International Congress and Symposium Series

Number 60

Driving and Epilepsy

– and other causes of impaired consciousness

Proceedings of an International Symposium sponsored by Labaz, held at the Queen's Medical Centre, Nottingham, on 25th June 1982

Royal Society of Medicine
International Congress and Symposium Series

Number 60

Driving and Epilepsy
– and other causes of impaired consciousness

Edited by

R. B. GODWIN-AUSTEN and M. L. E. ESPIR

Published jointly by

THE ROYAL SOCIETY OF MEDICINE
1 Wimpole Street, London

ACADEMIC PRESS
London Toronto Sydney

GRUNE & STRATTON
New York San Francisco

1983

ROYAL SOCIETY OF MEDICINE
1 Wimpole Street, London W1M 8AE

ACADEMIC PRESS INC. (LONDON) LTD.
24/28 Oval Road, London NW1 7DX

United States Edition published and distributed by

GRUNE & STRATTON INC.
111 Fifth Avenue, New York, New York 10013
Second Printing 1984

The sponsors of this Symposium are responsible for both the scientific and literary content of this publication. The Royal Society of Medicine has only sought to assure itself of the medical and scientific reputability of the work reported. The views expressed are not necessarily those of the Society. Distribution has been in accordance with the wishes of the sponsors but a copy is available free of charge to any Fellow of the Society.

Library of Congress Catalog Card Number: 83-70294
ISBN (Academic Press): 0-12-791617-2
ISBN (Grune & Stratton): 0-8089-1589-4

British Library Cataloguing in Publication Data

Driving and epilepsy. – (Royal Society of Medicine
international congress and symposium series; 60)
1. Automobile driving – Great Britain – Congresses
2. Epileptics – Congresses
I. Godwin-Austen, R. B. II. Espir, M. L. E.
III. Series
629.28'32 TL152.3

Typeset by Oxford Verbatim Limited
Printed in Great Britain by Whitstable Litho, Whitstable, Kent

Contributors

F. C. Edwards
Health and Safety Executive, Chapel Street, London, UK

M. L. E. Espir
Civil Service Medical Advisory Service, and Charing Cross Hospital and Northwick Park Hospital, London, UK

P. C. Gautier-Smith
Institute of Neurology, Queen Square, London, UK

R. B. Godwin-Austen
Queens Medical Centre and General Hospital, Nottingham, Regional Department of Neurology, Derbyshire Royal Infirmary, Derbyshire, UK

P. Harvey
Royal Free Hospital, Pond Street, London, UK

A. Hopkins
Department of Neurological Sciences, St Bartholomew's Hospital, London, UK

W. B. Jennett
University of Glasgow, Glasgow, UK

J. D. Parkes
Department of Neurology, Kings College Hospital, London, UK

M. Parsonage
The David Lewis Centre for Epilepsy, Alderley Edge, Cheshire and formerly of the Neurology Department, General Infirmary, Leeds, UK

P. A. B. Raffle
London Transport, London, UK

J. F. Taylor
Department of Transport, Orchard Street, Swansea, UK

P. J. Thompson
Institute of Neurology, Queen Square, London, UK

M. R. Trimble
Institute of Neurology, Queen Square, London, UK

Acknowledgements

The editors are grateful to Labaz for sponsoring the Symposium in Nottingham and this publication. Their gratitude is also extended to the Royal Society of Medicine for publishing the proceedings in this series. We also wish to thank the authors for all the work that has gone into the preparation of their contributions.

The editors wish to emphasize that they are not responsible for the opinions expressed nor the interpretations of the regulations in each chapter which are those of the respective authors.

Contents

Introduction

R. B. GODWIN-AUSTEN

Queens Medical Centre and General Hospital, Nottingham Regional Department of Neurology, Derbyshire Royal Infirmary, Derbyshire, UK

Many doctors, and especially family practitioners and neurologists, are called upon to advise patients about their fitness to drive following an attack of loss of consciousness. The regulations regarding driving licences for persons with epilepsy have recently been amended with effect from the 21st of April 1982 and are reproduced below. The detailed application of these regulations is often a matter of judgement and interpretation which sometimes results in patients being given conflicting advice by different doctors. This is amply illustrated in the chapter by Drs Harvey and Hopkins (pp. 9–15). Reports to the Driver and Vehicle Licensing Centre (DVLC) at Swansea are an expression of the doctor's opinion and the decisions of the DVLC are usually based on these opinions and medical records rather than a direct knowledge of the case. The aim must be to apply the regulations as Parliament intended and to achieve the highest degree of consistency and fairness in their application. This book reports the proceedings of a meeting held in the Queen's Medical Centre in Nottingham in June 1982. The meeting was called to provide the opportunity to discuss in detail aspects of the regulations relating to fitness to drive in patients with a history of loss or impairment of consciousness, from epilepsy and other causes.

ORDINARY DRIVING LICENCES FOR PERSONS WITH EPILEPSY

(1) The law provides for a driving licence to be granted if an applicant suffering from epilepsy satisfies the following conditions:–

- (a) he shall have been free from any epileptic attack during the period of 2 years immediately preceding the date when the licence is to have effect; or
- (b) in the case of an applicant who has had such attacks whilst asleep during the last 2 years, he shall have had such attacks only whilst asleep during a period of at least 3 years immediately preceding the date when the licence is to have effect; and
- (c) the driving of a vehicle by him in pursuance of the licence is not likely to be a source of danger to the public.

(2) The broad intention is to allow driving licences to be granted, in suitable cases, to people with epilepsy who have been free of any attacks for two years with or without treatment, or who have a history of at least 3 years of attacks only during sleep.

Driving and Epilepsy – and Other Causes of Impaired Consciousness, edited by R. B. Godwin-Austen and M. L. E. Espir, 1983: Royal Society of Medicine International Congress and Symposium Series No. 60, published jointly by Academic Press Inc. (London) Ltd., and the Royal Society of Medicine.

The regulations quoted above do not define what is meant by "suffering from epilepsy". Little difficulty arises where there is a history of a series of seizures. But a single epileptic attack – most would agree – cannot be considered to indicate a state of "suffering from epilepsy" and this has been recognized by advice from the Medical Advisory Panel that in the case of a solitary epileptic seizure a reasonable period of observation off driving is 1 year and occasionally 6 months. This matter is considered in greater detail in the chapter by Dr Espir. There is no reference to treatment in the regulations, in spite of the increased risk of recurrence of seizures when anticonvulsant drugs are stopped (about half the patients in the series reported by Juul-Jensen in 1964). The accepted but little publicized view (*Br. med. J.*, 1976) has been that driving should only be allowed if effective treatment is continued unchanged, and that any alteration of treatment should be followed by a period off driving for 6–12 months.

Gibberd and Bateson (1974) have cast doubt on the concept of a separate category of epilepsy where the attacks only occur during sleep. In such cases the risk of attacks during wakefulness always exists and the new regulations continue to insist on a history of attacks while asleep for a period of at least 3 years before driving is allowed. The assessment of whether someone suffering from epilepsy is "likely to be a source of danger to the public" is clearly a very subjective matter in many cases but the application of this condition (c) of the regulation is likely in practice to be relevant in epileptic subjects with low intelligence, psychological or neurological defects, and in those on drug treatment. There is a "grey area" of cases suffering two or more seizures in highly unusual circumstances, unlikely to recur; or in the setting of an illness such as encephalitis or meningitis. And in some cases of reflex epilepsy leniency in the application of the regulations may seem reasonable if the provocative cause of the attack is unlikely to occur during driving.

HEAVY GOODS VEHICLE AND PUBLIC SERVICE VEHICLE LICENCES

The law debars from driving a Heavy Vehicle or Public Service Vehicle any individual who has suffered an epileptic attack since the age of 5 years old.

The justification for stricter regulations for those driving heavy goods (HGV) and public service vehicles (PSV) is amply illustrated in subsequent chapters. Heavy goods vehicles are responsible for 70% more deaths than lighter vehicles. But the regulations may be criticized on a number of grounds. These licences are only required if the vehicle is driven on the public highway, and certain categories such as ambulances and taxis are not covered by the regulations. Employment which involves much driving, for example travelling salesmen, van drivers and delivery men are subject to the same regulations as those who may make only occasional use of their licence for social or pleasure purposes.

The diagnosis of a solitary attack of loss of consciousness in an applicant for an HGV or PSV licence may be difficult especially where there is an incentive for the applicant to falsify his history. The chapter by Dr Andrew Raffle illustrates how a large employer of PSV drivers can reduce accidents from this cause to a minimum by very careful medical supervision. But no such supervision can be provided for the majority of HGV drivers.

Driving is one of the most relevant and important skills of modern life. In the UK, 24 million – nearly half the adult population – are licence holders and for many the licence to drive is an economic necessity and an essential part of employment. It has been estimated that there are about 130 000 adult epileptics who are potential drivers, so that the size of the actual problem is very substantial. There have been those who have criticized the regulations by contrasting the case of epileptics with that of patients suffering from for example, heart disease. In this volume Dr Parkes discusses the topic of drowsiness, sleep and narcolepsy. Dr Taylor provides the statistical justification for epilepsy being singled out for specific legislation, and demonstrates that epilepsy is the major cause of collapse at the wheel causing a road traffic accident.

The number of cases considered by the Medical Advisory Panel on Epilepsy raises the question whether more specific regulations could be drawn up to reduce the "grey area" mentioned above. Unfortunately our knowledge of the natural history of patients who have had epileptic attacks is fragmentary, and it is therefore impossible to predict the likelihood of recurrent seizures. Similarly the statistics for the prospective risk of epilepsy following neurosurgical operations and head injuries is far from comprehensive. Professor Jennett contributes an important chapter on this subject and raises the difficult topic as to whether an individual with a high prospective risk of epilepsy should be subject to any special restriction of driving – especially if he is an applicant for an HGV or PSV licence.

Anticonvulsant drugs have effects on alertness, reaction time and driving skill. These effects may be exacerbated by associated medication and especially by alcohol. Dr Trimble has contributed an important chapter on this subject and his conclusions emphasize the importance of warning patients of the effects of drugs on driving skills.

The doctor who advises the patient about his fitness to drive carries responsibility in law. Thus a patient who is driving against the regulations but on his doctor's advice may reasonably claim that any damage that results is the doctor's responsibility. And similarly Motor Vehicle Insurance cover is not extended to those driving while medically unfit. Advice should only be given therefore after a most detailed and careful consideration of all the available facts. Corroboration of the history volunteered by the patient should be sought from medical records wherever possible since there may be a great temptation for the patient consciously to mislead and falsify his history. It should also be emphasized that a diagnosis of epilepsy should only be made when the clinical features support the diagnosis. The stigma of being diagnosed "an epileptic" with the added burden of ineligibility to drive is a disaster for someone who has suffered a benign and non-disabling attack of – for example – migraine or acute anxiety.

This book does not aim to provide answers to all the varied problems of the application of the regulations relating to epilepsy and driving. The booklet "Medical Aspects of Fitness to Drive" contains a chapter on Epilepsy and is circulated to all doctors as a guide. The recommendations contained in that booklet were made after widespread consultation and it is referred to by the DVLC in their work. The individual case may be discussed with or referred to the Medical Adviser at the Department of Transport, who may refer to its Medical Advisory Panel; finally the individual may appeal to the Magistrates Court. But hopefully improved communication between doctors working in this field will lead to greater consistency and fairness in decision-making, and to the public's readier acceptance of and therefore greater co-operation with the regulations on Driving and Epilepsy.

References

Gibberd, S. B. and Bateson, M. C. (1974). *Br. med. J.* **ii**, 403–405.
Juul-Jensen, P. (1964). *Epilepsia* **5**, 352–363.
Leading article. (1976). *Br. med. J.* **i**, 1235–6.

Epilepsy and Other Causes of Collapse at the Wheel

J. F. TAYLOR

Department of Transport, Orchard Street, Swansea, UK

Any person who precipitately collapses at the wheel whilst driving at speed is highly likely to be involved in major trauma and death. In these cases it is extremely difficult to determine at autopsy whether or not any scanty evidence of a seizure predated the accident and caused it or occurred secondarily as a result of head injury. It is therefore impossible to determine the part that medical factors play in many serious road traffic accidents.

However in those road traffic accidents where the trauma is less severe, we do have an opportunity to investigate the cause of the accident. This has been achieved in a series of 1605 police-reported accidents in which the driver survived and was minimally injured to the point that he could resume driving subsequently (Fig. 1). In this survey no less than 38% of accidents were due to a witnessed generalized seizure. "Blackouts" accounted for a further 23% of the cases and insulin-treated diabetes was responsible for 17%. Interestingly enough all forms of heart condition in aggregate accounted for only 10% and strokes only 8%, and this is especially important in view of the high incidence of these conditions in the community. A large number of the people who collapsed had failed to notify their condition to the Licensing Authority when applying for a driving licence. The law in Great Britain currently requires driving licence holders to notify any health condition which can affect safe driving either now or in the future unless it is not expected to last for more than 3 months. Of the people collapsing on account of witnessed generalized seizures, 70% had not declared their condition whilst 12% of this group were experiencing a first seizure.

Looking at the "blackout" cases in this series where all investigations proved negative and studying the age structure and case histories, it seems, on balance of probabilities, that at least half of these were probably epilepsy. A feature of the epilepsy cases was that the average age of collapse was in the region of 30 years whilst in the cardiovascular and cerebrovascular collapse cases, the mean age was over 40 years.

In the past it has been suggested that people who collapse at the wheel due to

Driving and Epilepsy – and Other Causes of Impaired Consciousness, edited by R. B. Godwin-Austen and M. L. E. Espir, 1983: Royal Society of Medicine International Congress and Symposium Series No. 60, published jointly by Academic Press Inc. (London) Ltd., and the Royal Society of Medicine.

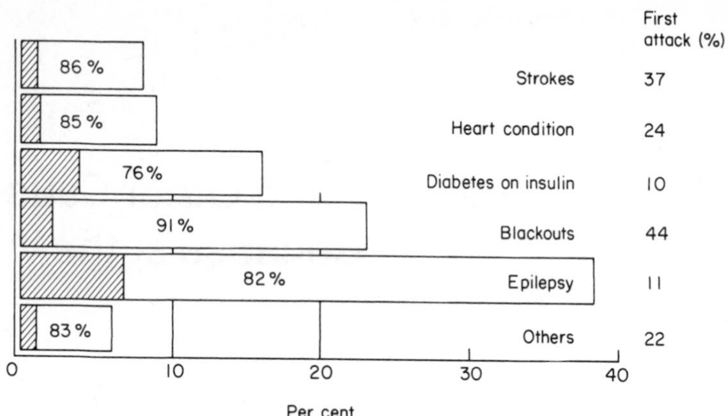

Figure 1. 1605 road accidents involving collapse at wheel, reported by the police DVLC (□ undeclared; ▨ declared).

epilepsy on average are not involved in serious accidents. This was certainly the impression in this series but of course we are not considering cases that are killed or maimed to the point that they can never return to driving. Most of the accidents in this series occurred at slow speed but in six cases the front passenger was able to take control of the vehicle and minimize the effects of the accident. Most of those surviving a collapse at the wheel with epilepsy had their accidents whilst travelling in restricted speed urban areas. One would expect that a person who suffers a seizure leading to altered or loss of consciousness whilst travelling on a motorway at speed, would be unlikely to survive.

An interesting feature when considering collapses at the wheel due to health conditions, is the third party motor insurance situation. A driver who is negligent, perhaps by crossing a double white line and causing an accident, is covered by his third party insurers who compulsorily have to meet the damages of third parties. However if a person collapses at the wheel on account of say epilepsy or a myocardial infarction, the third party motor insurers are under absolutely no obligation to meet any damages. This was illustrated by a Medical Defence Union case, some years ago, where a country cottage was seriously damaged as a result of a driver having a seizure at the wheel of a heavy goods vehicle. Third party insurers refused to meet damages and subsequent enquiries revealed that the driver had been granted a driving licence because a previous history of epilepsy had been concealed by the doctor completing the medical certificate form. It was later established that the doctor knew of this previous history and in consequence the doctor was accused of negligence, the Medical Defence Union settling the case by payment of an out of court settlement.

The second commonest group who collapse at the wheel are subjects with insulin-treated diabetes. Of 100 such cases reviewed 30% collapsed on account of a missed meal, 14% were on account of unusual effort. One of these cases involved a coal lorry driver who had to make an unusually large delivery to a private house. When he returned to his heavy goods vehicle, he had a hypoglycaemic collapse just after he started the diesel engine and put the vehicle into gear. The vehicle slowly moved forward, crushing a parked car in front and killing the two occupants, a doctor's wife and son. Diabetes treated with insulin is often mentioned as a prominent cause of collapse at the wheel but this was responsible for only 1% of the collapses in this series. So far as type of collapse is concerned, 3% manifested their hypoglycaemia by an epileptic seizure, 35% suffered from altered consciousness and 62% from complete loss of consciousness. Altered consciousness is I think a more menacing situation so far as driving is concerned than precipitate loss of consciousness. At least the latter results in the vehicle coming to an early halt but in the cases of altered consciousness in this series, one driver found himself at the wheel driving the wrong way up the M6 motorway being chased by a police car – he appeared to have driven for over 20 miles in the wrong direction. Another drove for over 24 miles the wrong way up a dual carriageway zig-zagging from side to side. An interesting feature of these cases was that they were able ultimately to be given sugar orally. One of the problems of altered consciousness in diabetics on insulin is that it tends to negate their training to take sugar. Some of the diabetics in this series described an overwhelming desire not to take the sugar which they knew they should take.

As mentioned previously, coronary thrombosis in this series accounted for only 10% of the collapses at the wheel but it is common knowledge that cardiac infarction is a prominent cause of accidents usually on account of death at the wheel. Death from cardiac infarction and also cerebrovascular accidents was readily determined at autopsy but on occasions it is impossible to determine whether or not the infarction ante-dated the accident and caused it or actually occurred in the throes of death from trauma. In conclusion therefore one has to say that it is impossible to determine the part that sudden death or collapse plays as a cause of road traffic accidents but that, reviewing the frequency of various conditions causing collapse at the wheel, epilepsy is certainly the front runner, probably associated with about half of these cases. Whereas cardiac infarction presents as a prominent cause of death at the wheel.

Neurologists, Epilepsy and Driving

P. HARVEY and A. HOPKINS

Royal Free Hospital, Pond Street, London, UK

There are good grounds for preventing some people with epilepsy from driving. The accident rate amongst *licensed* drivers with epilepsy has been shown to be between 1·3 and 2·0 times age-matched controls without epilepsy (Hormia, 1961; Waller, 1965). Accidents as a result of epilepsy which had not previously been disclosed accounted for 33 out of 43 accidents caused by seizures in one study (Millingen, 1976). Only two of the remaining accidents were caused by people who were driving legally under regulations similar to those in the United Kingdom, and the remaining eight resulted from first seizures. The importance of sensible restrictions is also shown in the same study. Of 205 drivers with declared previous seizures who were assessed for eligibility to drive, 122 were granted a licence, and none had a seizure in the period of follow-up. Eighty-three were initially ineligible, of whom 50 were eventually granted a licence. Five of these (10%) subsequently had a seizure, resulting in an accident, including the two cases noted above.

People with epilepsy are allowed to drive in Great Britain:

(i) If they have been "free from any epileptic attack while awake for at least three years from . . .", or,
(ii) "in the case of an applicant who has had such attacks whilst asleep but not whilst awake since before the beginning of that period", and,
(iii) provided the "driving of a vehicle by him . . . is not likely to be a source of danger to the public" (Motor Vehicles (Driving Licence) Regulations, 1981).*

Nobody may hold a Heavy Goods Vehicle (HGV) licence if they have had an epileptic attack after the age of 3 (Heavy Goods Vehicle Driving Licences) Regulations, 1977).

A doctor is obliged to remind his patient that he is "required by law to inform DVLC, Swansea, at once if you have any disability which is or may become likely to affect your fitness as a driver, unless you do not expect it to last for more than three months" (The Driving Licence), and to tell the patient if he thinks that the disability

* This survey was conducted before the introduction of the April 1982 Regulations.

Driving and Epilepsy – and Other Causes of Impaired Consciousness, edited by R. B. Godwin-Austen and M. L. E. Espir, 1983: Royal Society of Medicine International Congress and Symposium Series No. 60, published jointly by Academic Press Inc. (London) Ltd., and the Royal Society of Medicine.

will last more than 3 months. The DVLC then contacts the patient's general practitioner, and on his information (sometimes supplemented by information from the hospital physician) will make a decision on that patient's eligibility to hold a driving licence. Patients whose licence is revoked may appeal to the DVLC, which may consult an advisory panel of consultants.

We have become increasingly aware (1) of the number of "grey areas" into which our patients with epilepsy fall, (2) of seeming ambiguities in the law, (3) of inconsistent advice given by our colleagues to patients, and (4) of our inability to predict the DVLC's rulings in such "grey areas". In an attempt to identify the areas of confusion we circularized 233 neurologists (consultants and senior registrars) in the UK with a number of short case histories of patients with established or potential seizure disorders. They were asked to indicate the time at which they thought the subject of each case history would become eligible to hold a driving licence under the Driving Licence Regulations (1981). They were asked not to refer to the Regulations, but to indicate in their answers their understanding of them. They were also asked when they would prefer the patients to be allowed to drive if this differed from their interpretation of the official view. One hundred and thirty-two neurologists replied, a response rate of 56%.

A selection of the 23 questions is published below.

The questions

(a) A man of 51 has headaches for many years, but increasing diplopia led him to consult you. He had a sphenoid wing meningioma which was removed in a technically difficult operation. In the first 5 postoperative days he had three grand mal seizures, he was started on phenytoin and this was continued when he left hospital. You see him 5 months later in your clinic, and he has had no further seizures. Assuming he has no more seizures when may he drive?

(b) A bank manager of 55 consults you with his wife who tells you that her husband had a grand mal seizure at supper last week. He tells you that more than 30 years ago while in the army, the same thing happened whilst on parade. He has had no other seizures in the intervening years. Assuming he has no more seizures when may he drive?

(c) A housewife of 34 has two grand mal seizures within 1 h of each other, regaining consciousness and alertness between them. CT scan and EEG are normal. You see her 8 weeks later when she has had no further attacks and there are no physical signs. Assuming she has no more seizures when may she drive?

(d) An engineer of 40 had ten grand mal seizures between the ages of 10 and 22, when his medication was changed to phenytoin, 400 mg daily, and he had no more seizures. He holds a current driving licence. He is admitted to hospital for a minor surgical procedure, and the house surgeon orders his serum phenytoin to be estimated. This is 100 mmol/litre (25 ug/ml) (upper limit of "therapeutic range" 72 mmol/litre (18 ug/ml)). Despite there being no evidence of clinical toxicity, he reduces the dosage to 200 mg daily. Ten days later the engineer has a grand mal seizure while awake. He immediately goes back to taking 400 mg of phenytoin a day, and consults you 4 weeks later, having had no further seizures, and when his serum phenytoin is 100 mmol/litre (25 ug/ml). Assuming he has no more seizures when may he drive?

(e) A managing director had epilepsy for many years, characterized by grand mal seizures while awake but which have now been controlled with phenytoin for over

10 years. He holds a current driving licence renewed annually. He consults you with his wife who tells you that on four occasions in the last 6 months her husband has had grand mal seizures while asleep at three o'clock in the morning. Assuming he has no more seizures when may he drive?

(f) An insurance salesman aged 19 has his first grand mal seizure whilst awake at the office 2 months ago. Assuming he has no more seizures when may he drive?

(g) A woman of 45 is treated for depression with amitriptyline. Three weeks after beginning this treatment she has two grand mal seizures in the space of 3 days, one while asleep, and one while awake. Physical examination and investigation revealed no structural abnormalities of the brain. You see her in outpatients 1 month after the second seizure. She has stopped the amitriptyline. Assuming she has no more seizures when may she drive?

(h) The behaviour of a housewife aged 47 became strange and disinhibited over a period of 5 days. She then complained of a headache and then became increasingly drowsy. Examination of the cerebro-spinal fluid showed 23 lymphocytes per mm^3. Her EEG was diffusely abnormal. Over the next week she had three grand mal seizures. A diagnosis of encephalitis was made. It is now 3 months since the onset of her illness, she has made a complete recovery and one recent EEG has been normal. She has returned to her normal life. Assuming she has no more seizures when may she drive?

(i) A student of 19 consults you because he is embarrassed by his frequent myoclonic jerks. They began at the age of 12, occur within 1 h of awakening, and while he is nodding off to sleep. He has no other symptoms.

(i) His EEG is normal; when may he drive?
(ii) His EEG shows 3 Hz spike and wave activity. When may he drive?

(j) A municipal gardener of 37 has had epilepsy characterized by daily myoclonic jerks and weekly grand mal seizures from the age of 10. Five years ago he was put on sodium valproate since when he has had no generalized seizures but he continues to have myoclonic jerks within 1 h of awakening or while nodding off to sleep. This is now his only symptom.

(i) His EEG is now normal; when may he drive?
(ii) His EEG continues to show 3 Hz spike and wave activity, When may he drive?

(k) A van driver of 23 wishes to apply for an HGV driving licence. At the age of 18 months, 2 years and 4 years he had convulsions which were associated with high fever, but in every other respect he has been healthy. May he hold an HGV licence?

The answers

The replies are analysed in Figs 1, 2 and 3. The respondents understanding of the Regulations is displayed above the line and their expressed preferences below. A number of answers were not suitable for analysis in this fashion. The frequently occurring similarity between the understanding of the Regulations and the expressed preferences did not represent an equal number of "crossovers" in the replies. The questions may be divided into three main groups:

(A) Difficulties over the definition of epilepsy

A patient such as that in question (f), who has had a single seizure in the daytime can, in our experience, expect to lose his licence for a year. It is surprising to find that 28%

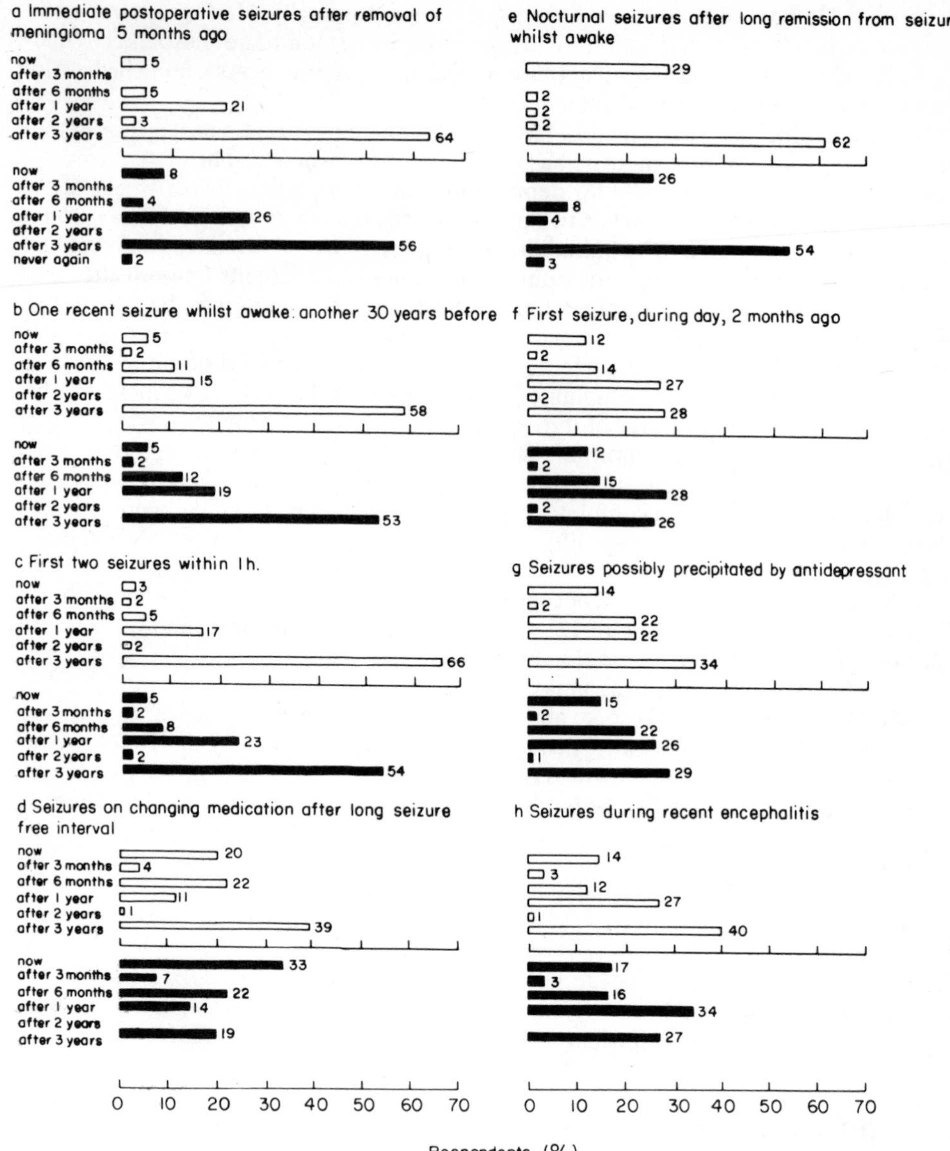

Figure 1. Eligibility to drive (■ expressed preferences; □ understanding of regulations).

of the respondents would expect the seizure to be treated by the DVLC as if it were epilepsy, and the patient would lose his licence for 3 years. Furthermore, only 2% less would have it otherwise. A rather alarming 12% would allow the patient to continue driving. In our view, two seizures occurring within 1 h of each other even if the patient is awake and compos mentis between them, could reasonably be considered as one epileptic event, and in our experience this has been the view of the DVLC. However, in question (c) 66% of our colleagues anticipated a 3 year ban, and 54% presented this as their preferred choice. Are seizures 30 years apart two

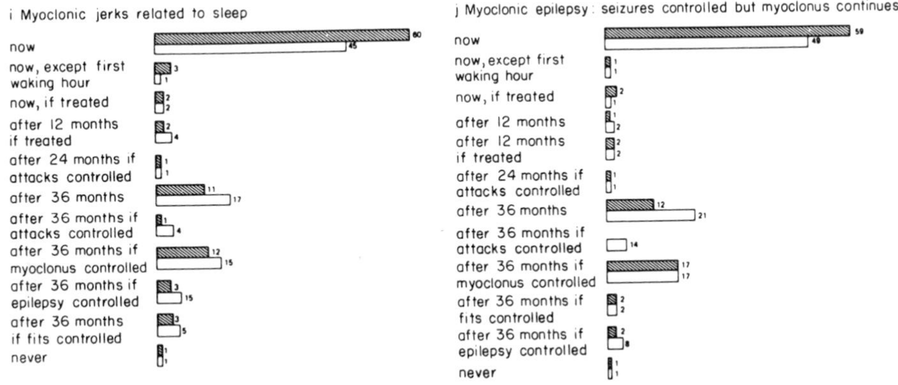

Figure 2. Eligibility to drive (▨ normal EEG; □ abnormal EEG).

individual events or do they comprise epilepsy? (question b). Are sleep related myoclonic jerks, with or without a history of seizures epileptic? Should the appearances of the electroencephalogram influence our definition? (questions (i) and (j)). The diagrams show the wide variation in the answers.

(B) Seizures precipitated in exceptional circumstances

Such a problem is seen frequently when medication is changed after a long seizure-free interval (question d). The answers were almost randomly distributed. Our experience of the DVLC is that patients have had to give up driving for a full 3 years after such an event, be it iatrogenic or not. This is patently unjust in many cases. Similar exceptional circumstances might be thought to occur in the problem of immediate postoperative seizures (a), antidepressant induced seizures (g), and after an encephalitis (h).

(C) Poor comprehension of the regulations

There are only two examples quoted here. The first is that of the man wishing to hold and HGV licence in question (k). We would not anticipate that he would ever be entitled to hold such a licence, although 17% thought he would be, and 24% thought he ought to be allowed to do so. The law relating to seizures while asleep is obscurely phrased and gives rise to much difficulty in practice. The person described in question (e) would in our experience be banned for 3 years, but nearly 30% of our colleagues thought otherwise. A slightly smaller number would prefer to let him continue to drive.

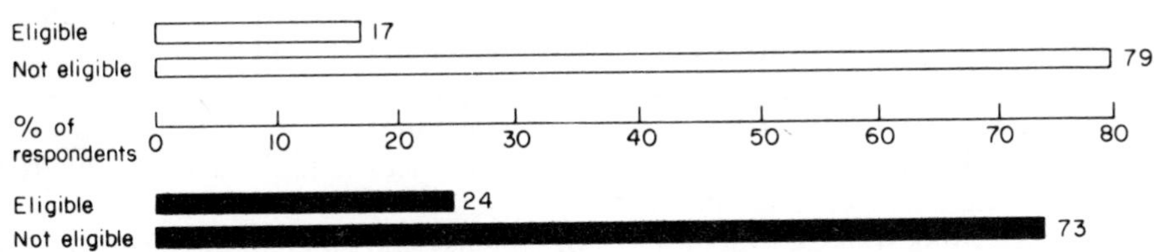

Figure 3. Eligibility to hold an HGV licence, after convulsions associated with fever aged 1 year, 2 years and 4 years (k).

Comments

The wide variation in our colleagues' understanding of the Regulations is both surprising and disturbing. It suggests that the Regulations are poorly understood, and in our experience erroneous advice is often given to patients with subsequent disappointment when the true position is explained to them. The rulings on individual cases given by the DVLC and the advisory panel should not in our opinion be regarded as law and can be disputed by appeal, but neither the guidelines on which the DVLC base their decision nor the advice given by their advisory panel are published. For example how widely is it known that the DVLC will stop a patient with epilepsy who is driving legally from so doing for 6 months after any change in his anticonvulsant therapy? In the absence of published advice from the DVLC, doctors turn to booklets (Pond and Espir, 1976) in which we think the advice is often misleading, which reflects the view of the authors, and which may be interpreted as having legal authority.

New regulations have been laid before Parliament,* but we are alarmed lest they lead to the same difficulties as the old ones. Gibberd and Bateson (1974) reported an annual continuing risk of development of attacks while awake in people whose epilepsy had started with sleep convulsions. The numbers are small after the first 3 years, but nonetheless there is a risk.

There is very good evidence for believing that many currently ineligible people with epilepsy are driving, and that they have concealed their epilepsy from the Licensing Authorities (Waller, 1965; Van der Lugt, 1975; Millingen, 1976; Hopkins and Scambler, 1977).

We would like to see a clear statement of Regulations for patients after they have had a single seizure. A recent study showed that 39% of people developed epilepsy after an initial seizure, (although people whose second seizure occurred within 6 weeks of the first were excluded from the study). The important point is that half of the patients developing epilepsy had their second seizure during the second year after the initial epileptic event (Cleland *et al.*, 1982). It would be infinitely more logical to ban driving for 2 years after the first seizure.

We suggest the following proposals be considered:

(1) A subject is ineligible to hold a driving licence for a period of 2 years after an epileptic seizure of any type, whether this occurred whilst the subject was awake or asleep. The Department of Transport has the discretion to extend the period of ineligibility on medical advice. The Department of Transport will also have the discretion not to extend the 2 year period of ineligibility in exceptional circumstances, eg:

- (a) if a second seizure occurs within 12 h of the first.
- (b) if seizures occur in relation to changes in or withdrawal of anticonvulsant medication after a seizure-free period of 3 years. In these circumstances, the subject will become eligible to hold a Driving Licence after a further seizure-free period of 6 months, provided that the previously successful anticonvulsant regime is restored.

(2) A subject is ineligible to hold a Driving Licence if his driving is likely to constitute a danger to the public.

(3) We think that clear definitions of epilepsy and an epileptic seizure should be included in the regulations:

* Introduced April 1982.

(A) Definitions

(i) A seizure is an abnormal, paroxysmal discharge of cerebral neurones clinically apparent either to the subject or to an observer. Unless there are clear precipitating factors of exceptional occurrence, all seizures, of whatever type, are presumed to be epileptic. Exceptions include:–

(a) a seizure resulting from cerebral anoxia (during syncope or during profound hypotension),

(b) insulin-induced hypoglycaemia,

(c) seizures occurring as an unwanted effect of drugs,

(d) seizures occurring only in association with fever, before the age of 4 years, and unaccompanied neurological signs. Such seizures are called "febrile convulsions",

(e) such other exceptions as may be defined from time to time.

(ii) Epilepsy is the occurrence of more than one non-febrile epileptic seizure of any type.

(B) Diagnosis

The diagnosis of epileptic seizure and epilepsy can be made by any registered medical practitioner, though the opinion of a Consultant Neurologist may be helpful. Investigations such as electroencephalography are not a prerequisite for the diagnosis.

We think serious consideration should be given to making epilepsy a notifiable disease. The principal objection against mandatory reporting of epilepsy by physicians is, of course, that this may prevent people with epilepsy seeking medical advice. It is also contrary to the accepted ethical position of respecting confidentiality between patient and physician. Nevertheless, such confidentiality is breached by the compulsory notification of certain infectious diseases; it could be argued that an unnotified driver with epilepsy was rather more dangerous than a notifiable child with scarlet fever.

The most striking thing about this study was the variation in understanding of the regulations concerning driving. Even in the simplest cases where there seemed to be clearcut guidelines a large number misinterpreted the regulations. When it comes to the "grey areas" confusion ruled. We think that there should be much clearer communication of the advice proffered to the DVLC by their advisory committee and that this advice should be published and circulated to doctors on a regular basis.

References

Cleland, P. G., Mosquera, I., Steward, W. P., Foster, J. B. Prognosis of isolated seizures in adult life. (1981). *B.M.J.* **283**, 1364.

Gibberd, F. B. and Bateson, M. C. (1974). *BMJ* **2**, 403–405.

Heavy Goods Vehicle (Driving Licences) Regulations, 1977.

Hopkins, A. P. and Scambler, G. (1977). *Lancet* **1**, 183–186.

Hormia, A. (1961). *Acta Psych. Scand.* Supp. **150**, 210–212.

Maxwell, R. D. H. and Leyshon, G. E. (1971). *B.M.J.* **3**, 12–15.

Millingen, K. S. (1976). *Proc. Aust. Assoc. Neurol.* **13**, 67–72.

Motor vehicles (Driving Licence) Regulations, 1981.

Pond, D. A. and Espir, M. (1976). "Epilepsy" *in* "Medical Aspects of Fitness to Drive" (Ed. Andrew Raffle).

The Driving Licence.

Van der Lugt, P. J. M. (1975). *Epielpsia* **16**, 743–746.

Waller, J. A. (1965). *N.E.J.M.* **273**, 1313–1420.

The Toxic Effects of Medical Treatment and Their Effects on Driving

M. R. TRIMBLE

The National Hospital for Nervous Diseases, Queen Square, London, UK

P. J. THOMPSON

Institute of Neurology, Queen Square, London, UK

Introduction

Motor car driving is a highly complex human activity. Perception of the environment has to be acted upon, quickly, and at any one time several different coordinated motor actions take place. Usually the journeys we travel are more than brief, and both concentration and vigilance are required to continue driving successfully. Medical conditions or drugs therefore, which impair any aspect of perceptuomotor skills, concentration or vigilance, may be expected to influence car driving and clearly may have potentially fatal implications. Although the relationship between taking psychoactive drugs and car accidents has repeatedly been speculated upon, in reality few studies have actually attempted to assess this. Most investigators interested in the area have, for obvious practical reasons, looked at the relationship between drugs and performance on a variety of tasks as can be measured in the laboratory setting. Typically, with respect especially to psychomotor performance, tests employed have included either simple tests of motor ability and coordination such as tapping ability, mirror tracing, card sorting or examination of performance on a pursuit rotor task, in which a stylus has to be kept in contact with a moving track or a revolving target. In such investigations, decrements in performance are noted for several groups of drugs, for example propranolol, diazepam and lorazepam (Ogle *et al.*, 1976), chlorpromazine (Kornetsky, 1976) and imipramine (Di Mascio, 1958). While interpretation of such data is complicated by consideration of attentional and motivational factors, they do suggest that drugs of the tricyclic antidepressant and tranquillizer groups may impair such performance.

Driving and Epilepsy – and Other Causes of Impaired Consciousness, edited by R. B. Godwin-Austen and M. L. E. Espir, 1983: Royal Society of Medicine International Congress and Symposium Series No. 60, published jointly by Academic Press Inc. (London) Ltd., and the Royal Society of Medicine.

With regard to car driving, studies have involved the use of either a driving simulator or real car driving and have suggested similar results. Clayton *et al.* (1977), for example, used a driving course laid out on a university car park. Subjects were asked to carry out specified tests in a Ford Escort saloon which included weaving in and out of bollards and a "gap acceptance task", in which a decision was made as to the feasibility of driving the car through a series of gaps. In these investigations imipramine was shown to have deleterious effects when compared with viloxazine or placebo. In the studies of Hindmarch (1977), a set of tests corresponding to basic driving skills were examined at a driving training centre. These were scored by officials from an advanced driving school and included steering between bollards, garaging and parking skills, and a break reaction time test. In his studies the benzodiazepines, lorazepam and diazepam, impaired performance more than clobazam. Of particular importance from such data is the suggestion of Hindmarch that significant correlations exist between brake reaction tests and laboratory assessed reaction time measures, suggesting some extrapolation from the experimental to the real-life situation.

In addition Hindmarch recommended the simple critical flicker fusion threshold (CFF) as an estimate of the sedation induced by a drug. In this test the flicker frequency of lights at which subjects can no longer discriminate between the flashes and report a continuous light, is noted, a low threshold being equated with sedation. Barbiturates persistently lower CFF (Hindmarch, 1982).

With this background, it is germane to consider two aspects with regard to the toxic effects of anticonvulsant treatment and their relevance to car driving. First, is there any evidence to suggest that these drugs impair psychomotor abilities, and secondly the practical effects of any observed deficits in a real-life situation?

The Effect of Anticonvulsant Drugs on Psychomotor Abilities

The main problem with many studies that have examined the influence of anticonvulsant drugs on any aspect of cognitive function has been the lack of control data and poor experimental design. For example, lack of a balanced crossover with placebo drugs or use of tests which are either subject to practice effects, or which are non-drug sensitive, being designed for the detection of structural rather than functional changes in the brain, confound interpretation of results.

In the literature there are no studies of anticonvulsants using the car driving simulator or actual car driving tests. In the laboratory, however, several have been examined using tests of reaction time, concentration and attention measures, CFF, and perceptuo-motor tasks that may have relevance for driving. A summary of the results from such investigations is given in Table 1. The studies have employed a variety of designs and tests, and several have used non-epileptic volunteers as subjects. As can be seen from the table, information about effects on several tests is incomplete and for some of the test classifications various results have emerged without consistency. An example here is the influence of sodium valproate on reaction time. While Sommerbeck *et al.* (1977), in 20 therapy-resistant hospitalized epileptic patients, noted increased reaction times and poorer tapping speeds, Harding *et al.* (1980) gave the drug to patients with photosensitivity and tested them before and after stabilization on an "optimum dose" of sodium valproate. Reaction time was significantly shorter on the drug. The results of Sommerbeck *et al.* may thus be the result of polytherapy and the pharmacological interaction between drugs, rather than an effect of sodium valproate *per se*. Similarly, Harding's data may reflect

Table 1
The effects of anticonvulsant drugs on selected tests of cognitive and motor ability

Drug:	Sodium valproate	Phenytoin	Carbamazepine	Phenobarbitone
Reaction time	Improvement (?)	Decreases	No effect	[a]
Attention	N	[a]	Improvement	No effect
CFF	N	N	No effect	Lowers
Perceptuo-motor skills	N	[a]	Improvement	Impairment

[a] Various studies show various results. N – Not tested.

changes in spike-wave activity, consequent on treatment which itself can alter reaction time.

In an attempt to provide further information on these important parameters, a series of investigations of the influence of anticonvulsant drugs on cognitive function and behaviour were carried out at the Institute of Neurology. More detailed information of these studies is given elsewhere (Thompson, 1981; Thompson and Trimble, 1981; Thompson *et al.*, 1981; Trimble, 1981) and here the investigations that may have relevance to car driving are reported briefly. At the outset it was our intention to develop a test battery which was sensitive to drug ingestion, free as far as possible from practice effects and seemed relevant to the clinical problems of patients with epilepsy. Volunteer studies were initiated with a view to eliminating the problem of seizures in the interpretation of results, but a balance was drawn between effects of drugs that may be transitory and longer-term effects, that are more likely to be a problem in the management of epilepsy, by using a 2 week verum, 2 week placebo crossover design. The influence of phenytoin (100 mg tds), carbamazepine (200 mg tds) and sodium valproate (1000 mg/day) on a variety of cognitive functions was assessed, and the results from tests of attention, perceptual speed, decision making speed and the motor response are shown in Table 2. Details of the testing schedule are given elsewhere (Thompson *et al.*, 1981). Attention was assessed using scanning tasks and the Stroop test; perceptual speed by noting the maximum length of time taken to recognize target items; decision making by presenting drawings of familiar items, asking questions regarding the item's category (e.g. is it living?) and recording

Table 2
Summary of the effects of anticonvulsant drugs on tests of possible relevance for car-driving ability

Drug:	Sodium valproate	Phenytoin	Carbamazepine
Attention – (Visual scanning)	L	L	
(Stroop test)		L	L
Perceptual speed			H
Decision making	L	L	
Visual motor response			L
Motor speed		L	

L – performance worse (significance $P<0{\cdot}05$ or greater); H – performance better.

the response time and accuracy. Finally a simple visual reaction time was used as the measure visuomotor response, and motor speed was assessed using a tapping task.

The results shown in the table suggest that phenytoin significantly impairs ability across all aspects of higher cognitive function, although in these investigations did not influence the visuomotor response. When correlation coefficients between serum levels of the drug, and change in scores between placebo and serum sessions were calculated, significant associations were noted, especially for perceptual speed and simple decision making tasks with greater impairment occurring at higher levels. The other two drugs impaired cognitive function less than phenytoin, in particular with regard to influences on perceptual and motor speed.

Generally, these results with volunteers are in keeping with the literature which has been reviewed elsewhere (Trimble, 1981) indicating that phenytoin has generally unfavourable effects on cognitive function and that some of the newer anticonvulsant drugs such as sodium valproate and carbamazepine are less toxic in this respect. This probably explains why patients changed from polytherapy onto, for example, carbamazepine show improvements in their cognitive function (Thompson and Trimble, in press), and why initiation of sodium valproate therapy in children was reported to improve school performance and attention (Jeavons and Clark, 1974).

Anticonvulsant Drugs and Car Driving Ability

As there are no tests that have directly assessed the influence of these drugs on car driving, extrapolation from the laboratory based studies reported must be interpreted with caution. The most persistent finding would seem to be the marked effect of phenytoin and the relative freedom of deleterious influence of sodium valproate and carbamazepine on perceptual and motor speed. It may be that this has significance less for routine driving than in a situation where rapid and immediate action is called for, such as in an impending collision. In other words, such studies may have more relevance for crashing and accidents than for driving *per se*. This is in accordance (a) with epidemiological surveys from several countries that have suggested that a causal link exists between the use of psychoactive drugs and traffic accidents, and (b) with the literature, suggesting a link between certain other CNS drugs and impaired performance on psychomotor tasks (Ogle *et al.*, 1976; Clayton *et al.*, 1977; Hindmarch, 1980; Trimble, 1981). The findings from such studies as these, however, have relevance for patients outside the field of epilepsy. Anticonvulsants are not simply and specifically "for convulsions". They are a heterogeneous group of drugs that act within the CNS which happen to be anticonvulsant, but which also have several other pharmacodynamic effects. They find use across a wide range of disorders from chronic pain, to heart disease, to anxiety, to, more recently, manic-depressive illness. Their growing use in patients who do drive emphasizes the need for further studies on their influence on both behaviour and cognitive function, and raises the question as to which are the most appropriate drugs to prescribe, and the nature of the warnings and advice that physicians prescribing such drugs should routinely be giving to their patients.

References

Clayton, A. B., Harvey, P. G. and Betts, T. A. (1977). *Psychopharmacology* **55**, 9–12.

Di Mascio, A., Klerman, G. L., Rinkell, H., Greenblatt, M. and Brown, J. (1958). *American Journal of Psychiatry* **115**, 301–317.

Harding, G. F. A., Pullen, J. J. and Drasdo, N. (1980). The effect of sodium valproate and other anticonvulsants on performance in children and adolescents. Sodium valproate in the treatment of Epilepsy. RSM International Congress and Symposium Series No. 30. Academic Press, London.
Hindmarch, I. (1977). *Br. J. clin. Pharmacol.* **4**, 1755–1785.
Hindmarch, I. (1980). *Br. J. clin. Pharmacol.* **7**, 189–1209.
Hindmarch, I. (1982). *In* "Advances in human psychopharmacology" (Eds G. D. Burrows and J. S. Werry), pp. 99–127. JAI Press, Connecticut.
Jeavons, P. M. and Clark, J. E. (1974). *Br. med. J.* **2**, 584–586.
Kornetsky, C. (1976). "Pharmacology". J. Wiley & Sons, New York.
Ogle, C. W., Turner, P. and Markomihelakis, H. (1976). *Psychopharmacology* **46**, 295–299.
Sommerbeck, K. W., Theilgaard, A., Rasmussen, K. E., Lohren, U., Gram, L. and Wulff, K. (1977). *Epilepsia* **18**, 159–166.
Thompson, P. J. (1981). The effects of anticonvulsant drugs on the cognitive functioning of normal volunteers and patients with epilepsy. PhD thesis, University of London.
Thompson, P. J. and Trimble, M. R. (1981). *Br. J. Pharmacol.* **12**, 819–824.
Thompson, P. J., Huppert, F. A. and Trimble, M. R. (1981). *Br. J. clin. Psychol.* **20**, 155–162.
Trimble, M. R. (1981). *In* "Current developments in Psychopharmacology" (Eds L. Valzelli and W. Essman), Vol. 6, 65–91. Spectrum, New York.

The Sleepy Driver

J. D. PARKES

Kings College Hospital, London, UK

Some causes of periodic and persistent day-time drowsiness which are clearly relevant to the problem of fitness to drive are listed in Table 1. The most common of these causes include a poor night's sleep, fatigue, alcohol and sedative drugs and the least common causes include disorders of excess day-sleep; the narcoleptic syndrome, essential hypersomnolence and sleep apnoea. No accurate figures for the prevalence of narcolepsy or sleep apnoea exist. However narcolepsy is not a rare disorder with perhaps 20 000 cases in the UK and 100 000 in the USA. Hypersomnolence is much less frequent with 2000 to 4000 possible cases in the UK. Sleep apnoea accounts for approximately 15% of patients presenting with day-time drowsiness (Guilleminault and Dement, 1977).

There are important variations in the pattern of day-sleep in patients with narcolepsy, hypersomnolence and sleep apnoea (Table 2). In all groups the usual trigger to day-sleep is any form of monotony or boredom and all patients may fall

Table 1
Some causes of day-time drowsiness

Insomnia at night	Anxiety
	Pain
	Depression
	Nocturnal myoclonus
	Sleep apnoea
Drugs and alcohol	
"Primary" hypersomnolence	Narcoleptic syndrome
	Essential hypersomnolence
	Narcolepsy alone
"Secondary" hypersomnolence	Encephalitis
	Head injury
	Cardiovascular disease
Periodic hypersomnolence	Kleine Levin
	Shift work

Driving and Epilepsy – and Other Causes of Impaired Consciousness, edited by R. B. Godwin-Austen and M. L. E. Espir, 1983: Royal Society of Medicine International Congress and Symposium Series No. 60, published jointly by Academic Press Inc. (London) Ltd., and the Royal Society of Medicine.

asleep with little or no warning. Attacks are more likely to be of sudden onset in sleep apnoea than in narcolepsy but both sudden-onset and gradual-onset sleep attacks can occur in the same patient with either disorder. Patients with hypersomnolence are persistently subwakeful rather than having frequent day-sleep periods. The degree of alertness between attacks is usually normal in narcoleptics. As in normal subjects, meals, fatigue, sedative drugs and alcohol increase the tendency to fall asleep in narcoleptics. Patients with narcolepsy are most sleepy in the evening, those with hypersomnolence in the morning.

Table 2

	Narcolepsy	Hypersomnolence	Sleep apnoea
Sleep attack duration (average–min)	20–30	120	1–5
Sudden attack with no warning	Unusual	Unusual	Common
Automatic behaviour	30–40%	40–50%	40–50%
Sleep drunkeness	Rare	Common	Occasional

Persistent and Periodic Excessive Day-sleep

Narcolepsy usually causes persistent life-long symptoms without any long period of remission, whilst in sleep apnoea the severity of symptoms may increase with age. The usual age of onset of narcolepsy and hypersomnolence is 15–25 and of sleep apnoea, 45–50. In contrast the outlook is different in subjects with the Kleine-Levin syndrome who usually recover eventually and in whom attacks of somnolence are periodic rather than sustained. This is also true in shift workers and flying crew in whom sleep is situational and predictable.

Automatic Behaviour and Sleep Drunkeness

These two conditions may occur in all disorders of excessive-sleep but are most common in essential hypersomnolence. During periods of automatic behaviour simple or routine tasks are accomplished normally and driving ability may be maintained despite patchy or complete subsequent amnesia for the period of attack. However, fatal accidents have been described during epileptic automatisms (Nanda, 1979).

Sleep drunkeness, subwakefulness with impaired motor control is a common event in hypersomniacs and usually occurs after waking from deep and prolonged sleep. Some degree of incoordination may last up to 1–2 h. This state will seriously impair driving ability (Guilleminault *et al.*, 1975).

Drowsiness and Driving

There is ample evidence that barbiturates, benzodiazepines, phenothiazines, tricyclic antidepressants, alcohol and other sedatives impair performance in driving tasks although the driver may be unaware of any impairment (*BMJ* **2**, 1415–7, 1978). Sedatives and antihistamines increase the risk of fatal accident at least five-fold whilst general anaesthesia may cause drowsiness, persisting for up to 3 days following minor surgical procedures (Routh, 1979). The evidence that day-time drowsiness as a result of disorders of excessive day-sleep rather than alcohol or drugs also impairs driving ability or is an important cause of road traffic accidents is less clear.

Sudden illness when leading to complete or partial loss of consciousness is a well recognized cause of accidents (Gratton and Jeffcoate, 1967). These authors discuss many acute and chronic medical conditions resulting in loss of awareness or sudden illness but do not include sleep attacks as a cause of road accidents. They conclude that the incidence of sudden or chronic illness as a cause or contributory factor to traffic accidents is low, around 0·5%. However, Bartels and Kusakcioglu (1965) reported that sleep attacks were a not uncommon cause of road accidents on the major highways in the eastern United States.

Driving Ability in Narcoleptics

A considerable amount of research has been done to establish the part that day-sleep attacks in narcoleptics may play in the causation of road accidents. Overall most reports are anecdotal (such as that of Kennedy, 1929), some are of uncertain reliability, and any control group is lacking. However there is no doubt that many people with narcolepsy have at some stage of their illness gone to sleep whilst driving and that drowsiness is at least occasionally responsible in these subjects for road accidents (Tables 3 and 4).

It is not clear to what extent, if any, subwakefulness rather than narcolepsy may be a contributory factor; or whether in people with the narcoleptic syndrome cataplexy and sleep paralysis may be serious risks whilst driving.

Treatment of narcolepsy with CNS stimulant drugs including amphetamine and methylphenidate will increase alertness and reduce the frequency of day-sleep attacks although only a minority of patients achieve total abolition of day-time drowsiness and up to a third of subjects rapidly become tolerant to amphetamines over the initial 1 to 3 months of treatment. Treatment of essential hypersomnolence with CNS stimulant drugs is usually not very effective and the medical treatment of obstructive sleep apnoea is unsatisfactory in most cases.

Table 3
Narcoleptic syndrome
patients who drive or have driven (64)

Gone to sleep whilst driving	48%
Had RTA due to sleep whilst driving	25%
Stopped driving because of narcolepsy	4%

Table 4
Narcoleptic drivers

	RTA with sleep	No RTA with sleep
	(16)	(48)
Age (mean and range)	46(22–70)	43(23–65)
Sex	11M 5F	27M 21F
On CNS stimulants	94%	82%
(Dextro Amphetamine: Mean and range, mg)	40(10–150)	35(10–120)
Severity narcolepsy (attacks/day: mean and range)	5·3(3–12)	4·1(2–10)
Automatic behaviour	40%	22%
Sleep drunkeness	25%	10%

EEG Diagnosis

In most patients with excessive day-time drowsiness, EEG polysomnography contributes little to the clinical diagnosis, which is usually obvious from the history alone. Although sleep-onset REM periods are common and may be diagnostic in narcolepsy, one or two normal day-sleep recordings do not exclude this diagnosis. The EEG is usually normal in subjects with hypersomnolence. The characteristic polysomnographic findings in a range of conditions are set out below:

(1) Narcoleptic syndrome	Short sleep latency (1–3 min) Sleep onset REM activity in 70–90% of subjects if recordings are repeated.
(2) Essential hypersomnolence	Short sleep latency (1–3 min) otherwise normal.
(3) Nocturnal myoclonus	Night sleep recordings may show repetitive tibialis anterior jerking.
(4) Sleep apnoea	EEG will differentiate central from obstructive types.

Physicians' Responsibility to the Sleepy Driver

Where the accused have no memory whatsoever of events prior to a car crash at a cross-roads, Lord Chief Justice Goddard entered this caveat; "that drivers do fall asleep is a not uncommon cause of serious road accidents and it would be impossible as well as disastrous to hold that falling asleep at the wheel was any defence to a charge of dangerous driving. If a driver finds that he is getting sleepy, he must stop." (Hill v. Baxter, 1958, 1 AER 193). A patient with narcolepsy may thus fail in his essential duty to stay awake. Driving ability in narcoleptics must depend on the severity and the frequency of attack, the degree of warning of impending sleep, the probability that such attacks may occur whilst driving, and the degree of symptomatic control by treatment.

With all these variables there can be no hard and fast rules as to driving ability of all patients with many different kinds of day-sleep disorders and each individual subject requires separate assessment. General guide lines in narcolepsy, sleep apnoea and hypersomnolence are suggested in Table 5. If there is any doubt as to driving ability and bearing in mind the high proportion of road traffic accidents shown in Tables 3 and 4, it may be in the patients best interest that they are advised not to drive.

Table 5

	Can drive?
Narcolepsy	
Off drugs	no
On treatment (good control)	yes
On treatment (poor control)	no
Sudden attacks	no
Idiopathic hypersomnolence	
Treatment usually ineffective	no
Patient subwakeful	no
Obstructive sleep apnoea	no
Kleine Levin	yes
Transient global amnesia	yes?

References

Bartels, E. C. and Kusakcioglu, O. (1965). *Lahey Clin. Found. Bull.* **14**, 21–26.
Editorial (1978). *Br. med. J.* **2**, 1415–7.
Gratton, E. and Jeffcoate, G. O. (1967). Medical Factors and Road accidents. Road Research Laboratory M.O.T. RRL Report LR 143.
Guilleminault, C. and Dement, W. C. (1977). *J. neurol. Sci.* **31**, 13–27.
Guilleminault, C., Billiard, M., Montplaisir, J. and Dement, W. C. (1975). *J. neurol. Sci.* **26**, 377–393.
Kennedy, A. M. A. (1929). *Br. med. J.* **1**, 1112–1123.
Nanda, R. N. (1979). *NZ med. J.* **90**, 193–5.
Routh, G. S. (1979). *Lancet* **1**, 673.

The Present Regulations and Their Application

M. L. E. ESPIR

Civil Service Medical Advisory Service, London, UK

In the preceding chapters much has been said about the grey areas and the undoubted difficulties that exist in dealing with certain types of cases. In this chapter I shall first recapitulate the amended regulations, and highlight the areas that should be clear and generally agreed, lest anyone thinks that the whole subject is shrouded in confusion.

The Amended Regulations

From 21st April 1982, an ordinary driving licence can be issued to someone suffering from epilepsy if the following three conditions are satisfied: (a) free from attacks – for 2 years; or (b) has had attacks only whilst asleep – for 3 years; and (c) driving is not likely to be a source of danger to the public.

In addition to the above, licence holders are required by law to inform DVLC Swansea at once "if you have any disability which is or may become likely to affect your fitness as a driver, unless you do not expect it to last for more than three months".

The regulations regarding Heavy Goods Vehicle (HGV = 7·5 metric tons laden) and Public Service Vehicle (PSV = nine or more seats for hire or reward) driving licences have also been amended (Road Traffic Act. The Heavy Goods Vehicles (Drivers' Licences) (Amendment) Regulations 1982). A person is now barred from holding a vocational licence if he: (1) has suffered an epileptic attack since attaining the age of 5 and (2) has any disease likely to cause the driving by him of a HGV or PSV to be a source of danger to the public.

Driving and Epilepsy – and Other Causes of Impaired Consciousness, edited by R. B. Godwin-Austen and M. L. E. Espir, 1983: Royal Society of Medicine International Congress and Symposium Series No. 60, published jointly by Academic Press Inc. (London) Ltd., and the Royal Society of Medicine.

Legal and Medical Fitness to Drive

Suffering from epilepsy is not defined in the regulations and we must remember that epilepsy is not a single disease entity. The law makes no distinction between the different causes or types of epileptic attacks, nor between their almost infinite variations in severity, frequency and precipitating factors. Furthermore not all attacks of loss of consciousness are epileptic. Some cases come into the category of "sudden attacks of disabling giddiness or fainting", which – like epilepsy – is a prescribed disability (Road Traffic Act, 1972, 1974) and a bar to driving. However legislation cannot cater for every eventuality and will not abolish all risks. Fitness to drive thus depends not only on the legal requirements, but is also a matter for medical judgement and careful consideration of each case on its individual merits. This is particularly true when dealing with an adult who has had a single fit.

The Importance of "Driving is not Likely to be a Source of Danger to the Public"

Condition (c) is particularly relevant for those on anti-epileptic drug (AED) treatment. To satisfy condition (c) and drive without being "likely to be a source of danger to the public", the following points should be considered for those on treatment: (1) they must obviously be free from unwanted drug effects which might impair driving ability, and (2) their freedom from fits may depend on continuing the same (effective) treatment regime.

Patients on satisfactory anti-epileptic drug treatment who satisfy conditons (a) or (b) should therefore be reminded that condition (c) also has to be fulfilled and that their safety and fitness to drive may be entirely dependent on their continuing the same treatment; and furthermore if they change or stop treatment, they must stop driving until advised by their doctor that it is in order for them to do so again (Leading article, *Br. med. J.* **1**, 1235–6; Raffle, 1976).

Sleep Epilepsy

If someone with a history of epileptic attacks whilst awake, starts having attacks only whilst asleep, driving will not be allowed – until either he has been free from all attacks for 2 years, or if attacks continue to recur whilst asleep, he shall have had such attacks only whilst asleep for at least 3 years immediately preceding the date when the licence is to have effect. In licence holders who have had epileptic attacks only during sleep for over 3 years, even if one attack – major or minor – occurs whilst awake, driving should be stopped and the licence holder must inform the DVLC. The possibility that sleep epilepsy may be symptomatic of an intracranial lesion and that other manifestations may develop also needs to be borne in mind. The term "nocturnal epilepsy" is best avoided as it is not necessarily synonymous with "sleep epilepsy". Not all nocturnal attacks occur during sleep, and attacks whilst asleep can occur during the daytime.

The First Fit – Is It Epilepsy?

Traditionally neurologists have taught that a solitary seizure is not necessarily indicative of epilepsy, as the term "epilepsy" should only be applied if there is a liability to recurrent attacks. The recent report from Newcastle (Cleland *et al.*, 1981) of 70 patients aged 16–65 followed up after a single witnessed major convulsion showed that 39% had subsequently developed epilepsy mostly within 2 years.* Thus, when a licence holder or applicant has a fit for the first time, whilst asleep or awake, driving should be stopped and clinical examination and appropriate investigations are necessary to try and identify the cause and assess the risk of recurrence. If there is clinical, EEG or other evidence of a primary cerebral cause, the liability to recurrence cannot be denied and the first fit should then be regarded as the equivalent of epilepsy. The licence holder is obliged to notify the DVLC and resumption of driving will be governed by condition (a) or (b) and (c).

There is also a group in whom a single fit does not justify the label of epilepsy. For example:

(1) Attacks resembling epilepsy may be due to a cardiac disorder (Schott *et al.*, 1977), and thus have a syncopal basis. They would then be classified as "sudden attacks of disabling giddiness or fainting", and driving would probably not be allowed until there has been freedom from attacks for a year (Raffle, 1976; Oliver and Somerville, 1980).

(2) There may be evidence of exceptional precipitating factors which are not likely to recur or can be avoided (Daneshmend and Campbell, 1982).

In these cases, if there is no evidence of any other cause, then it may be considered that there is no disability for the ordinary licence holder or applicant to declare to the DVLC. However, driving should be stopped pending specialist advice, and it is suggested that the doctor writes personally to the Medical Adviser at the DVLC seeking the opinion of the Honorary Medical Advisory panel, without disclosing the patient's name unless consent is given.

There remains the difficult problem of those who have a solitary seizure without any significant provocation and clinical examination and investigation fail to reveal the cause. They thus have *no evidence* of a liability to recurrence, but in view of the uncertainty and risk of recurrence, the licence holder or applicant should notify the DVLC. Private driving in these circumstances would probably not be allowed for at least 12 months and employment as a driver, particularly as a vocational driver, should be suspended indefinitely. Follow-up is very important and if there is a recurrence or if other evidence of a cerebral disorder develops, then the conditions applying to epilepsy will operate.

* Further information on this topic has been published since the Symposium, emphasizing that patients with first seizures are not homogeneous in terms of risk of epilepsy. Hauser and his colleagues (*New Engl. J. Med.* (1982) **307**, 522–8) studied 244 patients after a first unprovoked seizure categorized as idiopathic, acute symptomatic and remote symptomatic. They showed that the frequency of recurrence ranged from 14–50% at 2 years. A positive family history, a generalized spike-wave electroencephalographic pattern and a history of prior neurological insult increased the risk of recurrence after a first unprovoked seizure.

Symptomatic Epilepsy

Patients who have one or more fits due to a structural intracranial lesion should not be allowed to drive until there has been freedom from attacks for 2 years. In some whose condition resolves rapidly (e.g. due to encephalitis) or after successful neurosurgery (Jennett, this volume, p. 49) the risk of fit recurrence may be considered to be small and such cases may be referred to the Honorary Medical Advisory Panel. Most, if not all, will be treated with AEDs, but there is little uniformity as yet in the advice given regarding the duration of treatment (Clarke, 1980; Leading article, *Lancet* (1980) **1**, 401–2; North *et al.*, 1980; Richardson and Uttley, 1980). The risk of fit recurrence if AED treatment is withdrawn also needs to be considered, and if driving has been resumed on satisfactory treatment, it may be safer to continue the same treatment indefinitely.

Some patients following head injury (Jennett, 1975) and others after certain neurosurgical operations have a high risk of developing epilepsy (Jennett, this volume, p. 5). Prophylactic AED therapy may be prescribed and in these high risk cases at least 1 year without fits should elapse following the operation or injury before private driving is allowed. The attitude towards withdrawing treatment should then be as outlined above. In such cases, HGV and PSV driving should not be allowed, even though they have had no fits, and employment driving other vehicles (Edwards, this volume, p. 46) would also be inadvisable.

In view of the wide variation in risk of developing epilepsy according to the site and nature of the lesion, the type of injury and early complications, fitness to drive in each case should be assessed individually.

As a general rule, no one with a malignant or inoperable intracranial tumour should drive, even if no fits have occurred, although there may possibly be rare exceptions – for example with evidence of "cure" and 2 years or more without fits – in whom private driving may be considered.

Likewise it is recommended that patients with lung cancer even if apparently successfully treated should not drive professionally because of the risk of epilepsy due to cerebral secondaries.

Medical Management and Advice to Patients

Licence holders are obliged by law to inform the DVLC if they become aware that they suffer from a prescribed, relevant, prospective or limb disability, or a disability which has already been notified to the DVLC but has become worse, unless the disability is not expected to last for more than 3 months. The onus is on the licence holders to notify the DVLC of any condition likely to make their driving a source of danger to the public, and in many cases they will be dependent on their doctor's advice. Although some will not heed advice and will disregard the regulations, nevertheless many are prepared to be sensible and comply, and it clearly is important that doctors advise their patients appropriately. If those with a history of epilepsy satisfy the prescribed conditions and are permitted to drive a private vehicle, they should be advised to avoid driving for many hours at a time and to take extra care not to go for long periods without food or sleep, and employment as a driver is not advisable (Raffle, 1976). With regard to confidentiality, doctors should observe the code of professional conduct and not breach confidentiality except exceptionally, i.e.

only if judged to be in the best interests of the patient or the public, and only after every effort to obtain the patient's compliance or consent has failed (Handbook of Medical Ethics, 1981).

References

Clarke, P. P. R. (1980). *Lancet* **1**, 650.
Cleland, P. G., Mosquera, I., Steward, W. P. and Foster, J. B. (1981). *Br. med. J.* **283**, 1364.
Daneshmend, T. K. and Campbell, M. J. (1982). *Br. med. J.* **284**, 1751–2.
Jennett, W. B. (1975). "Epilepsy after non-missile head injuries." Second edition. Heinemann, London.
Leading article. (1976). *Br. Med. J.* **1**, 1235–6.
Leading article. (1980). *Lancet* **1**, 401–2.
North, J. B., Penhall, R. K., Hanieh, A., Hann, C. S., Challen, R. G. and Frewin, D. B. (1980). *Lancet* **1**, 384–6.
Oliver, M. and Somerville, W. (1980). *Health Trends* **12**, 86.
Raffle, A. (1976). Medical aspects of fitness to drive. Third edition. Medical Commission on Accident Prevention, London.
Richardson, A. E. and Uttley, D. (1980). *Lancet* **1**, 650.
Road Traffic Act (1972 and 1974). HMSO, London.
Road Traffic Act. The Motor Vehicles (Driving Licences) (Amendment) (No. 3) Regulations 1982. Statutory Instrument No. 423.
Road Traffic Act. The Heavy Goods Vehicles (Drivers' Licences) (Amendment) Regulations 1982. Statutory Instrument No. 429.
Schott, G. D., McLeod, A. A. and Jewitt, D. E. (1977). *Br. med. J.* **1**, 1454–7.
The Handbook of Medical Ethics. British Medical Association (1981), London.

The HGV/PSV Driver and Loss or Impairment of Consciousness

P. A. B. RAFFLE

London Transport, London, UK

Available evidence suggests that the medical condition of a driver, with the exception of the effects of alcohol, is not an important factor in road accidents. Many drivers accept their doctor's advice and either do not drive, or restrict their driving within the limitations of their disability. Indeed, the latter may be an important reason why medical conditions do not often appear to be a factor in serious crashes. For instance, the casualty rate per 1000 persons for car drivers is more than 2·5 times greater in the 20–29 age group than in the 50–59 age group. Yet, as Havard (1973) has pointed out, it is in the younger group in which the various bodily functions thought to be important in driving, eyesight, reaction time, etc., are at their best. The age groups which incur the least risk of accident are those in which medical conditions are most likely to occur, and in which the faculties are already subject to the degenerative processes of advancing age. Ysander (1973) has suggested that this is partly due to a voluntary restriction on driving by older drivers with conditions likely to affect it. The same may well apply to many of those who are under treatment for conditions which can cause collapse at the wheel. They heed advice from their doctors.

It is difficult to estimate the extent to which unfitness to drive actually contributes to road accidents. Grattan and Jeffcoate (1968) in the United Kingdom and Ysander (1970) in Sweden both suggested that actual illness in drivers was responsible for only 1–2 per 1000 road accidents. It must be remembered, however, that neither study included as "illness" temporary factors like tiredness or the effect of drugs; and we can only estimate subjectively to what extent emotional, personality or behavioural abnormalities and any treatment for them, not amounting to illness, can contribute to accidents.

The transport and Road Research Laboratory (1977) in-depth study of accidents produced some interesting results on these subjects. The study was based on interviews and questionnaires of survivors of accidents. Therefore, to some extent, the allocation of causation, or contribution of a factor to the accident was subjective, though great care was taken to eliminate as many uncertainties as possible. The

Driving and Epilepsy – and Other Causes of Impaired Consciousness, edited by R. B. Godwin-Austen and M. L. E. Espir, 1983: Royal Society of Medicine International Congress and Symposium Series No. 60, published jointly by Academic Press Inc. (London) Ltd., and the Royal Society of Medicine.

study, based on the assessment of drivers involved in 2130 accidents, indicated that the following partially or mainly contributed to the accidents:

Fatigue	7·5%
Illness	1·5%
Emotional Distress	1·2%
Medication	4·0%

compared with 1–2 per 1000 of actual illness in the other studies. The difference of approximately ten-fold between illness and actual illness in the different studies is one of definition. In the one, illness or feeling unwell being one of possibly several factors contributing to the event, and in the others, actual illness causing the event.

When profession drivers alone are considered the contribution of illness to road crashes is very small indeed. Over 25 years we recorded the incidence of acute illness at the wheel among London Transport bus drivers, in order to determine what medical conditions led to potential or actual accidents and hence to place the medical surveillance of bus drivers on a rational basis. We have defined acute illness at the wheel as a medical condition causing the driver to collapse at the wheel or to feel so unwell that he had to stop his bus not at an authorized bus stop. Data for the 25 years up to the end of 1977 (Table 1) shows that over the period there were 127 incidents of acute illness at the wheel of which 59 led to accidents. Data for the 4 subsequent years have not yet been fully analysed, but there have been 12 further incidents none of which were attributed to probable epilepsy and only two of which resulted in accidents.

An accident includes anything from a scrape of paint off a vehicle to a multiple fatality. Taking into account the 7·4 thousand million miles driven in the period, this amounts to one incident of acute illness every 64 million miles driven and one accident every 130 million miles driven. London Transport drivers are, of course, highly selected; they are self-selected in wishing to drive and in continuing to drive a bus in London (those who have frequent accidents leave the job) and are further selected by medical surveillance before and during employment. I would like to

Table 1
London transport – Diagnoses in cases of drivers acutely ill at the wheel 1953–1977 inclusive

Diagnoses	No. of incidents	No. of incidents in which collision or other accident occurred
Acute ischaemic heart disease	34	8
"Hypertension"	5	2
Cerebrovascular accident	4	1
Transient cerebral ischaemia	6	2
Ruptured aorta	2	0
Vasovagal attack or simple faint	21	12
Probable epilepsy	24	17
Loss of consciousness of uncertain origin	14	10
Hypoglycaemia	5	2
Laryngeal vertigo	2	2
Miscellaneous	10	3
Total	127	59

Total man years – 406 000; total miles driven – 7 410 400 000.

make three points about the causes of these incidents and accidents. Acute ischaemic heart disease was the commonest cause of acute illness at the wheel but led to very few accidents. The 24% of the acute ischaemic heart disease incidents which resulted in accidents contrasts with the 60% of vasovagal attacks and 70% of probable epilepsy and of loss of consciousness of uncertain origin which led to accidents. Perhaps the percentage of incidents of epilepsy which led to accidents should be increased to 80% because in two of them a probable accident was prevented by the intervention of others. In one, the woman conductor of a single deck bus steered the bus to safety and in the other a police officer jumped on to the side of the bus and applied the brake. But we must stick to our definition.

We have tried to be precise in our allocation of the events to the diagnostic groups, and this largely explains why so many cases of loss of consciousness remained classified as of uncertain origin in spite of the most exhaustive investigations. It is likely that this group contains cases of possible epilepsy, some possible vasovagal attacks and a few that can only be classified as falling asleep at the wheel.

So far as the seriousness of the accidents is concerned they varied from the trivial to the worst bus accident experienced in London Transport, when eight potential passengers waiting in a bus queue were killed when a bus driver collapsed at the wheel. The collapse was attributed to a vasovagal attack. One collapse attributed to acute ischaemic heart disease killed two other road users. There were four other fatalities, two of which were attributed to cases of epilepsy.

Turning now to the 24 cases attributable to probable epilepsy, seven of the cases were aged between 22 and 30 in which there were five accidents, six aged between 31 and 40 in which there were three accidents, five were aged between 41 and 50 with four accidents, three were aged between 51 and 60 with two accidents and three were aged 61 to 65 with three accidents (Table 2). Taking into account the 406 000 man years of experience in the 25 years study, making broad estimates, using the age distributions over the years, based on complications used in our sickness absence studies over the last 35 years we can estimate that in the 22 to 30 age group there was one incident approximately each 11 300 man years of experience, in the 31 to 40 age group one case in every 14 500 man years, in the 41 to 50 age group one case every 19 800 man years, in the 51 to 60 age group a case every 35 000 man years, in the last group one case every 11 400 man years (Table 2).

Even with such small numbers, there is a hint of a selection and/or self-selection effect with an increase in the 60's possibly attributable to epilepsy secondary to other pathology.

All this has to be put into the perspective of the surveillance of London's bus drivers over and above the requirements of the PSV Regulations. London Transport

Table 2
London transport 1953–1977 – Drivers acutely ill at the wheel due to probable epilepsy

Age	No. of cases	No. of accidents	Man years of driving per case
22–30	7	5	11 300
31–40	6	3	14 470
41–50	5	4	19 760
51–60	3	2	34 957
61–65	3	3	11 377
Total	24	17	

drivers are medically examined on entry to the occupation; at each public service vehicle licence renewal following the 46th birthday and 5 yearly thereafter, with an extra examination at 62 or 63; after 21 days of absence attributed to sickness or accident; after failure to complete a shift because of illness; after absence from work of any duration attributed to vertigo, diseases of the heart and blood vessels, epilepsy, eye disease or eye injury and diabetes; and at any time at the request of management, of the driver, of the driver's doctor or the London Transport occupational physician. At each of these medical examinations, the driver completes a medical questionnaire, one of the questions being "have you ever at any time in your life suffered from blackouts, epilepsy, fainting or attacks of giddiness?"

Of course there is concealment. I can see no way around the problem. Of the 24 cases, we have evidence of concealment from other sources, apart from the patient in five cases, three out of the six in the 31 to 40 age group. One extraordinary case was aged 52, with 27 years service who had managed to conceal his epilepsy for the whole of that time. One was a 27-year-old bus driver in whom I had signed the original PSV medical certificate. Three weeks after coming out of training as a bus driver he had a fit at the wheel and killed a motorcyclist in the Buckingham Palace Road. Subsequent enquiry by the police showed that he had been a known epileptic since the age of 15. I would suggest that suspicion should be raised when an applicant for a PSV licence goes, without good reason, to any other doctor but his own for the completion of the medical certificate. Occupational physicians have some advantage in doing these examinations because they are adept at obtaining an occupational history. They also have the advantage that very often an employment department will bring back a reference from a former employer which does not give a completely clean bill of health or it contains ambiguous phrases about health. One of my former colleagues, now retired, a very courteous man, always helped a patient off with his jacket in these cases which gave him the opportunity to give the jacket a gentle shake in order to listen for the rattle of tablets in a bottle.

Of course, these are not the only cases of epilepsy which have been diagnosed amongst current bus drivers. A driver on duty does not spend all his time driving, but he is often under surveillance because he also uses London Transport canteens and clubs. Off duty he will perhaps have an advantage as it is usually more difficult to get clear-cut eye witness account of the episode where the driver has an event which might be epileptic. One of the cases of epilepsy occurring at the wheel is of particular interest. It occurred in a man aged 62 and led to an accident in which a pedestrian was injured. It turned out to be the first manifestation of a cerebral secondary and that was the first manifestation of his carcinoma of the lung. We have at least three other cases of carcinoma of the lung presenting as epilepsy in bus drivers but, fortunately, in none of them were they driving at the time.

Four other cases of interest, three aged between 58–60 in which their fits appeared to have been precipitated by hypoglycaemia. Another one aged 59 turned out to have intermittent atrial fibrillation: investigation suggested that his late-onset epilepsy was due to cerebral embolism, and he subsequently developed typical grand mal.

In those cases in which the diagnosis is firmly established we have no option in the handling of the case but we still try to find alternative work for those who have been with us for some years. Of course we do not feel so sympathetically disposed towards those who have deliberately concealed their condition on entry to the Service. Equally there is very little difficulty in those cases which are categorized as loss of consciousness of uncertain origin. We may suspect epilepsy but that is not the point. From the public safety aspect an employer would be vulnerable if he continued to employ, as a bus driver, someone who had already demonstrated he had had such an acute illness at the wheel. We have our quota of doubtful cases. We go to great lengths to make sure we get all the available information, with the patient's consent. At the same time we try to use the same sort of criteria for decision as they do at the Driver and Vehicle Licensing Centre. Perhaps we have the same sort of problem as that body does where they find sympathy overrides the facts. There is the same problem with alcohol dependency.

To sum up, the law requires higher standards of physical and mental fitness for vocational drivers because what would be appropriate for the driver who occasionally drives a car at weekends would be quite inappropriate for the bus (PSV) or lorry (HGV) driver who drives all his working day (and is therefore "at risk" for far longer); who finds it difficult to stop driving if he feels unwell; who drives mainly on urban routes where there are many more people and other vehicles to collide with; and who has a much heavier vehicle which will do more damage in a crash than a car. Bus drivers are at special risk because they have to stop repeatedly at places where people queue to board them and the consequences of loss of control of the vehicle can be very serious indeed. On the other hand the "professional" driver has much more experience in how to avoid the pre-crash situation and in dealing with the unexpected emergency.

The transport industry has its own tougher standards than the law requires but still cases of collapse or impairment of consciousness at the wheel occur. One can only speculate what might happen without this surveillance.

References

Grattan, E. and Jeffcoate, G. O. (1968). *Br. med. J.* **1**, 75.

Havard, J. D. J. (1973). Proceedings Public Works Congress 1972, 482–585.

Transport and Road Research Laboratory (1977). A Preliminary Survey of the Role of Drugs Other Than Alcohol in Road Accidents. Leaflet LF 677. Transport and Road Research Laboratory.

Ysander, L. (1970). *Acta. Chirurg. Scand.*, Suppl. 409.

Ysander, L. (1973). Elderly Male Automobile Drivers in Gothenburg and their Traffic Behaviour in the Year 1971. IDBRA Cong. Zurich.

Employment as a Driver in Persons with a History of Epilepsy

F. C. EDWARDS

Chapel Street, London, UK

This chapter is not concerned with HGV/PSV driving, or taxi driving, where the situation on fitness, medical examinations and review for licensing is very similar, but will cover certain aspects of employing someone to drive "as an occupation". This is usually called "professional" driving, in distinction to "vocational" driving, a term used mainly for the former groups.

Four aspects are covered. First, medical advice on epilepsy and professional driving, second the role of Occupational Health Services; third the Health and Safety at Work Act and EMAS. Finally, some aspects of driving certain vehicles on ground other than the public highways.

Epilepsy and Professional Driving

There are two contexts for advice on employment as a driver. First, career advice to those who already have epilepsy and, secondly, advice to those who develop epilepsy while established in an occupation.

For the first category we would definitely not advise either taking up any occupation or career which was heavily driving dependent, or driving as a main occupation. If there is a continuing liability to seizures, in other words if epilepsy is established, occupations involving much driving are not generally suitable. Secondly, if epilepsy develops in someone established in a certain occupation, each case would be settled *ad hoc*, depending on the individual and on the actual job. Close liaison between the consultant and the occupational health physician is desirable. These decisions must take into account the type of epilepsy, the time of seizures, the degree of control and any precipitating factors.

In the first context, we advise that professional driving is *not* a suitable occupation for any one with a history of epilepsy. The reasons are obvious: driving time overall is increased, there may be long periods of driving without a break, and the individual

Driving and Epilepsy – and Other Causes of Impaired Consciousness, edited by R. B. Godwin-Austen and M. L. E. Espir, 1983: Royal Society of Medicine International Congress and Symposium Series No. 60, published jointly by Academic Press Inc. (London) Ltd., and the Royal Society of Medicine.

will have to drive when he may not feel like it, rather than at times of his own choosing. He may have to drive with a mild intercurrent infection or other illness which, while insufficient to keep him off work, might impair his seizure control. Occupations where a substantial part of the day is taken up with driving duties (such as chauffeurs and sales representatives) are very inadvisable.

However, there is no statutory bar to driving vehicles (other than heavy goods, public service vehicles or taxis) as an occupation, provided that the individual holds a current driving licence. The ability to drive is often an economic necessity. We know that a substantial proportion of current driving licence holders have epilepsy and that some professional drivers have a history of epilepsy. Therefore, espcially in our second context, we have to be realistic and acknowledge the need for informed advice to the individual.

In the ideal situation, we know that the individual definitely has epilepsy; we know his full seizure history; we know his medication, which is optimal and free from side-effects; and there are no other associated conditions, physical or psychiatric, that would impair driving. These features must all be taken into account when the assessment is made. If the physician advising about suitability for driving, whether an occupational physician or an Employment Medical Adviser, considered that the diagnosis was uncertain or the management of seizures could be improved, then the individual would of course be referred back for further consultation.

In general, we would fully support the advice given in the latest edition of "Medical Aspects of Fitness to Drive", (Raffle, 1976) bearing in mind the recent changes in the regulations, and also Parsonage's advice to Tyrer's "Treatment of Epilepsy", published in 1980. In particular, the following advice would be offered to those entitled to drive under the regulations:

(1) If on the same treatment for a 2-year period, with no day time attacks during this period, then some driving duties would be allowed, and the medication should continue.

(2) Those on treatment must always remain under medical supervision and treatment should continue unchanged while driving. Medical advice to the individual should cover both the taking of other medication and alcohol and a note should be made of any side-effects likely to impair driving skills.

(3) If medication is altered, reduced, or discontinued, then driving duties must be stopped and 6 months should elapse before a decision is taken. The majority of seizures recur within 6 months of reducing or changing medication and this period should be sufficient.

(4) Should any further day time seizures occur, all driving duties must of course be stopped immediately and cannot be resumed until the individual is again eligible for a driving licence.

(5) If a professional driver with no history of epilepsy develops seizures, then he must immediately discontinue all driving and be referred for investigation, diagnosis and treatment. Driving duties are discontinued until he becomes eligible again for a licence, when the individual case history will be reviewed for a decision on resumption of driving duties.

The above points emphasize the great importance of keeping accurate occupational health records. If one of the main components of the job is driving, there is likely to be an initial health screening and/or health declaration at recruitment or transfer. Where there is an Occupational Health Service there should be a method of alerting it to occurrences that might affect fitness for driving, so records systems must incorporate means of notification and review. Health review should be done following sickness absence and, in the case of an employee with epilepsy, after any absence, however long, and at regular intervals. Many large firms now would be advised by their Occupational Health Physicians, that the employee with a history of epilepsy who was eligible for a current driving licence would be allowed to drive a car or light van for part of the day, provided there were no other circumstances affecting his fitness to drive.

In such firms there may be occasional needs for staff on duties not normally requiring driving, to drive the firm's vehicles for short periods. In order to cover these possibilities, occupational health staff should be alerted so that health reviews may be made, as individuals recruited for non-driving duties may not have full health screening initially.

There is a grey area where the job itself is not a professional driving task but the individual, though not driving a vehicle owned by the firm, has to use his own car at times, e.g. travelling to inspect, visit or supervise. Here, the health status of the employee would have been covered for the employer if a health declaration had been made and is also covered through the possession of a driving licence because the individual has a duty to inform the Department of Transport of relevant disabilities.

Resettlement

If driving has to be stopped, large companies and firms may be able to transfer employees to other work, but if the individual with seizure development or recurrence is with a small employer, or the only jobs available are those he can not do safely, he may lose his job.

Services are available from the Manpower Services Commission which can help. The DRO can advise patients about prospects and may obtain suitable work. If further assessment is needed, this can be undertaken at an Employment Rehabilitation Centre (ERC – there are 27 throughout the country) as knowledge of other aptitudes may be needed. Our organization, the Employment Medical Advisory Service, provides medical and nursing services to the ERCs, where we see 14 000 clients per year, of whom 5% have epilepsy. For a quick assessment patients may be referred directly to one of our doctors. In job introduction and job rehearsal schemes, work suitability may be assessed on the employers premises: these are available through the DRO.

The Manpower Services Commission has reconsidered the question of registration as a disabled person and of the quota scheme. The new proposals, which are not yet agreed, would lay a duty on employers to take reasonable steps to promote equality of employment opportunity for disabled people. The legislation would be linked to a code of practice which would give employers practical guidance. This would cover both recruitment and retention of disabled people and encourage full and fair opportunities for career development. The principle that a certain proportion of the work-force should be disabled might be retained. These recommendations will expand the scope of the law to cover disabled people within work, as well as those seeking work, and should enlarge opportunities for the newly disabled who have to leave certain jobs. The new law would apply equally to all disabled people.

Occupational Health Services

There is no duty to provide Occupational Health Services. Although such services have existed for many years, over a third of the workforce is still not covered (Table 1),

Table 1
Distribution of Occupational Health Services

87·6% of firms, covering 36% of work-force, employ no medical or nursing staff
2–3% of firms, covering 44% of work-force, employ both medical and nursing staff

From EMAS Survey, 1976.

particularly smaller firms (Table 2). Services may be provided in a number of ways.

An Occupational Health Service's function is to safeguard the health of the work-force. Where hazards are low and the likelihood of occupational disease is remote there is no need for a regular system of health checks, but basic personnel records should be kept on all employees. Where work (e.g. driving) could affect the safety of others, more detailed records should be kept, particularly of illness, injury and absences. If the employee has temporarily to leave a specific job (e.g driving duties) for health reasons, then surveillance should be continued, to monitor the medical condition and also to make decisions about a suitable time for return to the work or to alternative work.

In many jobs, one of which is professional driving, there is benefit in pre-employment health screening and periodic reviews of health. These are particularly important on return to driving duties after sickness absence. It is the function of occupational health staff to advise management on the suitability of the employee for the particular work, without disclosing confidential medical information. The decision on employment must be for management to make.

If medication of a patient with epilepsy is altered the occupational health physician, if there is one, as well as the family practitioner, should be informed. Sometimes the first indication that occupational health staff may get of a change in therapy, is when an employee, who has had no seizures for many years, suddenly has one. Indeed, this may be when the illness, although long standing, is first manifest to the employer: although occupational health staff may have known of the condition for some time, they may not have needed to recommend any change or modification of the job to management. Disclosure to occupational health staff (OHS) should only be made with the consent of your patient. Such consent may already have been obtained in writing when a health declaration is signed by your patient at the recruitment stage.

Table 2
Distribution of Occupational Health Services

No. of employees in firm	% of firms without OHS
Under 25	Over 90
25–99	80–90
100–249	66
250–499	39
500–999	15
1000+	less than 10

From EMAS Survey, 1976.

Specific Examples of Good Occupational Health Practice

Health screening with a questionnaire or health declaration will be undertaken, usually by an occupational health nurse. Medical examination will only be necessary in certain circumstances and may be decided on after scanning the health form. If an employee suddenly develops seizures, the OHS will be notified, the employee would then be seen and, after medical assessment, management would be advised on the effect which the medical condition had on the particular job, which may need either altering or modification, and on driving duties.

Good practice, when considering the employment of people with epilepsy, would be that each individual's medical history would be looked at in the context of the job concerned. The decision on job placement would be made after the full medical history was taken into account. In many firms there would be no absolute bar to the employment of someone with epilepsy in any other occupation than heavy goods vehicle driving or work at heights. People with epilepsy who are eligible for an ordinary driving licence would, in many circumstances, be considered fit for employment in a wide range of different work.

If there are occasional day time seizures the employee would not be allowed to handle dangerous machinery or to work at heights and of course may not drive on the roads. If employed in a safer type of work, and if he consents, his co-workers should be told of his problem and of what to do if a seizure occurs. Occupational health staff should be in touch with the consultant and/or the general practitioner, about the patients management. The individual should never be labelled just as "epileptic" but the confidential health records should describe the history properly with a specific mention of the type of seizure, its characteristics and treatment.

It is appropriate to mention, at the end of this section, that when advizing on employment and epilepsy, we tend to use eligibility for a current driving licence as a yardstick for suitability for a variety of types of employment. I am not talking about such jobs as crane driving or other particularly hazardous occupations. But, if we wish to reinforce our advice to prejudiced employers who may be reluctant to consider placing someone with epilepsy in a situation which we feel is not a hazard, then this is a very logical standard to use.

Health and Safety at Work

Under the HSAWA (1974) both employer and employee have responsibilities for health and safety at work (Table 3). Of the two complementary aspects, the effects of work on health and of health on work, covered by the Act, it is the latter with which we are concerned here. The *employer* could be in contravention of the Act (both as far as his own employees and the general public are concerned) if he knowingly assigns an employee with a medical condition, to a job where this condition could expose him, or others, to exceptional risk. The duty on *employees* can be taken to include a duty to make known to his employer any physical or mental condition which might affect his ability to perform the work in question safely. It is the responsibility of the employee to make such a condition known if he is aware of it, to the employer. The occupational physician has a responsibility both to the employee and to management. He cannot break medical confidentiality and disclose the individual's medical condition to the employer without the consent of the employee,

Table 3
Health and Safety at Work Act

Section 2
(1) It shall be the duty of every employer to ensure, so far as is reasonably practicable, the health, safety and welfare at work of all his employees.

Section 7
It shall be the duty of every employee while at work –
(a) to take reasonable care for the health and safety of himself and of other persons who may be affected by his acts or omissions at work.

but he can and should state to management "this individual is fit/unfit" for the particular duties or job concerned.

Patients must be encouraged to disclose their condition to their employer where there are possible hazards at work. This may be thought detrimental to employment prospects and there is evidence that people are disclosing less with rising unemployment. However, there is also some evidence that disclosure is more likely to lead to retention and promotion than is concealment, in enlightened and responsible companies.

Dismissal on medical grounds is likely to be judged by a tribunal to be *fair* if the employee concerned has knowingly concealed his condition and made false statements about it; and also if full and frank discussion of the condition and of the way in which it might affect the job concerned, have taken place between employee and employer. Dismissal on medical grounds is likely to be judged *unfair* if the employer dismisses, having recruited and/or assigned the individual employee in the knowledge of his existing condition; and also if dismissal occurs without any prior discussion with the employee.

There has been concern that the passage of the Act may have made it more difficult for people with conditions such as epilepsy to get work. However, we know of no reliable evidence that this is so: on the contrary, raising of safety standards, better guarding of machinery, are likely to make prospects better.

The Employment Medical Advisory Service (EMAS) is an organization with a field force of doctors and nurses, working in 10 regions throughout Great Britain. It is the medical arm of the Health and Safety Executive. Our functions are to help prevent ill health caused from work and to advise those with health problems on suitable work. We advise the Manpower Services Commission and also provide doctors and nurses for the 27 Employment Rehabilitation Centres, and keep in close touch with consultants over individual cases where possible.

Other Types of Vehicles and Driving

The scope of this book has been mainly concerned with driving on the roads. However, industry uses numbers of powered vehicles driven within factory and construction sites, container terminals and on agricultural land (farming and forestry). These vary in size from small dumpers and lift trucks, to larger lift trucks, tractors and the substantial vehicles used with containers. There are eight categories of lift trucks alone and vehicles used in container terminals range from small and medium trucks to the huge straddle carriers, where the cab is high above the ground. There are about half a million tractor drivers and about the same number of truck drivers in this country.

There are several points about driving such vehicles. First, drivers can drive these without a licence, unless they drive them outside the site concerned, in which case they must be in possession of an ordinary driving licence or of a specific licence, e.g. a tractor licence. Second, accident statistics are available, but there is little or no evidence that accidents have been caused by pre-existing medical conditions, partly because such evidence has not been specifically sought.

Third, there is no statutory provision requiring medical examination for drivers of these vehicles. However, this does not affect the employers rights to include such a provision in their employees contracts.

Therefore, medical criteria and standards are not laid down consistently throughout the country. Where these have been made, they are likely to be (a) general recommendations on what is good practice, from Government, experts or the industry concerned; (b) standards laid down by a particular company for application in respect of their own employees by their own occupational health staff, both on recruitment and transfer. Both these types of recommendations will be adapted and modified from time to time.

We must also remember two further factors. Firstly, large numbers of these drivers work for small employers without occupational health staff and, secondly, in some situations drivers may transfer from small vehicles to larger ones and there may be difficulties where different standards are used for different categories of vehicle.

Standards of medical fitness for different occupations and for drivers of different vehicles will develop from an expressed need by the industry concerned and would normally be drafted following discussion between the industry (employers and unions), its industrial training boards or committees, occupational health physicians working for the industry, the Health and Safety Executive, medical advisers to the TUC and the Industry Advisory Committee if relevant.

Any such medical criteria or guidance on health screening would normally emerge as recommendations. We have already contributed to the revision of simple guidance on health screening and medical standards for both lift truck drivers and drivers of vehicles in container terminals. In making our recommendations for lift trucks, and for vehicles driven in container terminals, we think the standard needed for current driving licences is reasonable for drivers of small lift trucks, but that the much stricter standards needed for heavy goods vehicle drivers should be applied to drivers of the large straddle carriers and side loaders. In both instances however we emphasize that each case must be carefully assessed individually by occupational health staff or other medical advisers. Where there is right of transfer to the larger vehicle, the stricter standard should be applied.

The final question mark is in the voluntary application of agreed medical standards and health screening recommended as good practice where there are no statutory regulations. It is important that such recommendations take into account not only health and safety but also economic aspects, and should avoid being too restrictive unless there is very good reason.

References

The Health and Safety at Work etc. Act, 1974, Chapter 37. Department of Employment, HMSO, London.

"Medical Aspects of Fitness to Drive" (Ed. P. A. B. Raffle), 3rd edition, 1976, (reprinted 1978). Medical Commission on Accident Prevention, London.

Occupational Health Services, The Way Ahead, 1977. Health and Safety Commission, HMSO, London.

Parsonage, M. (1980). "The Treatment of Epilepsy", (Ed. J. H. Tyrer), p. 313. MTP Press Ltd, Lancaster, England.

Epilepsy After Head Injury and Craniotomy

B. JENNETT

University of Glasgow, Glasgow, UK

Cerebral trauma, accidental or surgical, is now one of the commonest causes of acquired epilepsy in the working age group in Westernized countries. Current regulations for driving focus on the risk of a further fit once epilepsy has been diagnosed. However, there is often hesitation in reaching this diagnosis when fits have occurred in exceptional precipitating circumstances, among which recent head injury or craniotomy are sometimes cited. On the other hand, some patients recovering from recent brain damage can be identified as at risk of developing epilepsy, even though no fit has as yet occurred; they have a "prospective disability". For these reasons the application of the regulations to patients who have had head injury or intracranial surgery often gives rise to controversy (Editorial, 1980).

There are now extensive statistics about the risk of epilepsy after head injury, and these draw a distinction between early and late traumatic epilepsy (Jennett, 1975). In the first week epilepsy has several distinctive features: fits are much commoner in the first than in the next few weeks, they are often limited to focal motor twitching, without becoming generalized, and less than a third of these patients with early epilepsy go on to have further fits in the future.

The risk of *late* epilepsy varies from 1% to over 60% according to the type of injury and early complications. Factors that predispose to late epilepsy are an intracranial haematoma that is surgically removed within 2 weeks of injury, the occurrence of early epilepsy, and a depressed fracture of the skull vault (Table 1). The risk of epilepsy after a compound depressed fracture of the vault varies widely according to various risk factors – whether the dura is torn, there is more than 24 h PTA, there are focal neurological signs of cortical damage or there has been an early fit (Fig. 1). In patients who have neither a depressed fracture nor an intracranial haematoma, the risk of late epilepsy is only about 1%, even if there is prolonged PTA, unless there has been an early fit. In that event it is 22% when PTA is less than 24 h and 30% when it is longer. The significance of early epilepsy for the future is similar when there has been only one fit in the first week as when there have been repeated seizures; and whether these were focal or general; and whenever in the first week they occurred.

Driving and Epilepsy – and Other Causes of Impaired Consciousness, edited by R. B. Godwin-Austen and M. L. E. Espir, 1983: Royal Society of Medicine International Congress and Symposium Series No. 60, published jointly by Academic Press Inc. (London) Ltd., and the Royal Society of Medicine.

Table 1
Factors influencing incidence of late epilepsy

	Factor Absent			Factor Present			
	Total	No. with late epilepsy	(%)	Total	No. with late epilepsy	(%)	*P*
Haematoma	854	27	(3)	128	45	(35)	<0·001
Early epilepsy	863	29	(3)	238	59	(25)	<0·001
Depressed fracture	832	27	(3)	694	104	(15)	<0·001

Data about the frequency of epilepsy after craniotomy are now beginning to emerge from several authors (Gautier-Smith, 1970; Cabral *et al.*, 1976a, 1976b; Editorial, 1980; North *et al.*, 1980; Richardson and Uttley, 1980; Foy *et al.*, 1981). There are variations in the duration of follow-up, and in whether early post-operative epilepsy is included or not – but nonetheless the figures are sufficiently consistent to indicate an overall risk of about 20%. As with head injury there are certain circumstances in which risks are considerably greater. These include certain pathological conditions, such as cerebral abscess, ruptured middle cerebral artery aneurysm and intracerebral haematoma complicating subarachnoid haemorrhage. Whatever the condition the risk of epilepsy is much greater when there has been epilepsy either pre-operatively or during the first post-operative week. The relative contributions of the surgical procedure and the underlying condition to the genesis of epilepsy is difficult to assess in any one case, but there is good evidence that the additional brain damage that is an inevitable consequence of supratentorial surgery is an important factor (Cabral *et al.*, 1976b; North *et al.*, 1980). Whether improved surgical techniques (such as use of the operating microscope) will reduce the risk of epilepsy remains to be seen. Greatly improved early surgery for missile injuries, with a much lower infection rate, has not had any effect on the frequency of late epilepsy in successive wars (Worlds Wars I and II, Korea and Vietnam).

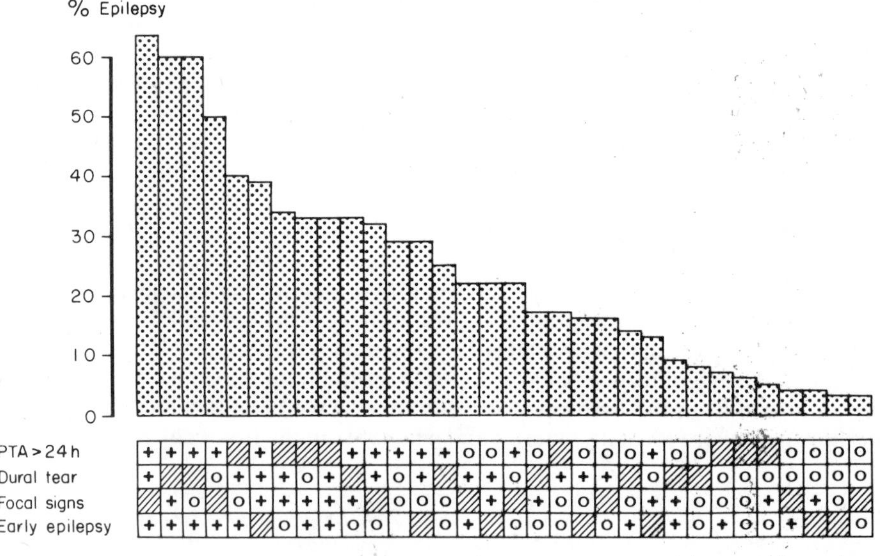

Figure 1. Late epilepsy after compound depressed fracture (three factors known).

Given that after traumatic brain damage, whether accidental or surgical, the likelihood of epilepsy can be estimated, the question is what advice should be offered to patients about anticonvulsants and about driving. A survey of over 1000 American neurosurgeons in 1973 revealed great variation in practice and that 40% of surgeons never prescribed prophylactic drugs – because they were uncertain which patients were at risk (Rappaport and Penry, 1973). The authors suggested that many Americans were suffering unnecessarily from traumatic epilepsy because of lack of therapy. A recent survey of 55 British neurosurgeons, representing most units in the country, shows that the proportion of them who routinely prescribe anticonvulsants after various kinds of surgery, corresponds approximately with the ranking of risks reflected in published studies. More than half the surgeons considered that drugs should be prescribed even when the risk of epilepsy was less than 10%, and rather less than half considered that this level of risk justified a temporary ban on driving a private vehicle. Two-thirds considered that driving of heavy goods or public service vehicles should be disallowed at a lower level of risk than that applying to a private vehicle.

Although some surgeons have protested that craniotomy carries a low risk of epilepsy, especially when carried out for lesions on the surface rather than in the brain, this survey shows that most neurosurgeons do recognize that their patients have a liability to fits after surgery. How effective anticonvulsants are in preventing epilepsy after traumatic brain damage is uncertain, but several trials are currently being conducted. Until these have reported favourably it would seem prudent to advise patients not to drive for 6–12 months after certain types of head injury or after craniotomy for any condition, and for longer if they are in one of the high risk groups.

References

Cabral, R. J., King, T. T. and Scott, D. F. (1976a). *J. Neurol. Neurosurg. Psychiat.* **39**, 1052–1056.

Cabral, R. J., King, T. T. and Scott, D. F. (1976b). *J. Neurol. Neurosurg. Psychiat.* **39**, 663–665.

Editorial (1980). *Lancet* **i**, 401–402.

Foy, P. M., Copeland, G. P. and Shaw, M. D. M. (1981). *Acta Neurol.* **55**, 253–264.

Gautier-Smith, P. C. (1970). "Parasagittal and falx meningiomas." Butterworths, London.

Jennett, B. (1975). "Epilepsy after Non-Missile Head Injuries." 2nd Edition. Heinemann, London.

North, J. B., Hanieh, A., Challen, R. G., Penhall, R. K., Hann, C. S. and Frewin, D. V. (1980). *Lancet* **i**, 384–386.

Richardson, A. E. and Uttley, D. (1980). *Lancet* **i**, 650.

Rappaport, R. L. and Penry, J. K. (1973). *J. Neurosurg.* **38**, 159–166.

Problem Cases of Epilepsy and Driving

P. C. GAUTIER-SMITH

Institute of Neurology, Queen Square, London, UK

Most patients when attending for a medical consultation start out with the basic assumption that the doctor is on their side and accept that this is so even when the advice given is unpalatable. However, where epilepsy and driving are concerned, they often believe the reverse to be the case. Although the majority of people are prepared to accept the fact of not being allowed to drive with good grace if the situation is clear-cut and it is obvious that they would be a danger at the wheel, this is not always so and such remarks as: "it's not fair"; "my life will be ruined"; "I will lose my job"; "plenty of people are driving with worse fits than mine"; "I always get plenty of warning" may be made. Clearly, in the grey areas, particularly if the attacks are minor, a patient may understand the advice even less well and may feel even more resentment.

If patients are to respect the law and report their attacks and in order to help them to accept decisions revoking their licences, it is essential that time is taken both for explanation and discussion. It might be worth pointing out, for example, that a car has hardly been used for a long time and is merely being kept as an extremely expensive gesture of independence, taxis and hire-cars can be used with the money saved, wives and husbands can do the driving, lifts can be arranged and so on. A GP, who had had three major seizures within the space of 3 months, was very resentful at losing his licence, saying that he wouldn't be able to continue his work and that he would have to give up medicine. Fortunately, a serious cause for his fits was not found, control of the attacks proved a simple matter and at the end of 3 years, he had the good grace to write to say that he had coped easily by the use of a bicycle, his wife driving on occasions and by reorganizing his practice, all of which had led to a healthier, more relaxed life and even an improvement in his marriage. Problem cases as they present to the Advisory Panel on Epilepsy may be conveniently considered under a number of headings.

Driving and Epilepsy – and Other Causes of Impaired Consciousness, edited by R. B. Godwin-Austen and M. L. E. Espir, 1983: Royal Society of Medicine International Congress and Symposium Series No. 60, published jointly by Academic Press Inc. (London) Ltd., and the Royal Society of Medicine.

The Patient

At medical consultations, one usually sets out with the premise that the patient is telling the truth, but where epilepsy and driving are concerned, this is by no means always the case. One example was a man who obtained medical certificates to be off work with the complaint that he was having blackouts, but when his HGV licence was threatened, claimed that he had never had them, despite the evidence of his GP's referral letter and the hospital records.

On several other occasions, patients have changed their stories dramatically from one consultation to another. In one case, a woman attending a neurological clinic gave a history on which a confident diagnosis of temporal lobe epilepsy was made – she had complicated aura followed by loss of consciousness. With her licence under threat, she asked for a second opinion and went to see another equally reputable neurologist, to whom she gave a completely different history. On reading both sets of case notes, it was difficult to believe that they were referring to the same patient. A further case was that of a young man wanting to train as an HGV driver, who claimed that he had made up a story of blackouts in the past as a "kid's way of getting out of school".

On a few occasions, the reverse situation has occurred in which a patient has preferred to accept the consequences of pleading guilty to a charge of careless driving rather than admit that he had had a collapse at the wheel. An example was a doctor who sought a neurological consultation because he had lost consciousness while driving and had hit another car. The likely cause was thought to be a fit secondary to cerebral vascular disease and as he had had a collapse at the wheel, he was advised to report it and warned that it was likely that a 6–12 month period off driving would be the consequence. A short time later, he pleaded guilty to a careless driving charge, saying to the court that he had been preoccupied and had not been paying proper attention. He was fined £50 and his licence was endorsed.

The Doctor

Many doctors feel uneasy when there is a conflict between what they see as the patient's interest and the law, particularly if they consider that regulations are unfair. This can be perfectly understandable, but on occasions this point of view may be carried to extremes and ignorance of the law may give rise to ill feeling. A man had two nocturnal seizures, 3 months apart and when his doctor was informed that the patient's licence was going to be revoked, he wrote back: "I feel that the present legislation is unreasonable and that the grey area of uncertainty should always be interpreted to the patient's advantage." In fact, there was no uncertainty – no one was disputing that the patient had had two major convulsions while asleep – and the law is not grey in that particular situation.

A further point that crops up from time to time both with patients and their doctors is the concept that they are being unfairly penalized for being honest. A letter was received from a doctor in support of a patient. "As you well know, there are many people suffering from poorly controlled epilepsy who are still driving and who failed to report their medical condition to the Department of Transport. On the other hand, we have a situation such as that of Mrs. . . . who has been completely honest about the situation. Because of this I feel that she is at present being unnecessarily penalised." No argument was advanced that the evidence as to epilepsy was ill founded, nor that the regulations had been wrongly interpreted and if the rule of law is to be upheld, such a viewpoint is surely indefensible.

Medical Problems

Minor attacks

In some countries, the regulations do not apply if minor attacks occur without loss of awareness. However, in law it is very difficult to define "impairment of consciousness" and sometimes, despite a patient's assurance that they have been fully conscious throughout an attack, EEG and video evidence combined makes it quite clear that this is not the case. A young man had had major fits until 1977, when they stopped, and he merely complained of minor dizzy feelings, which he claimed did not interfere with anything he was doing. An attack was recorded on video and simultaneous EEG and during it, he stopped what he was doing for about 20 s and during that time was immobile and unresponsive. Clear after-discharges of an epileptic type were seen on the EEG.

The correct diagnosis of minor symptoms in the context of previously documented epilepsy can be very difficult. A woman aged 25 years had had partial complex seizures frequently going on to major fits and at the age of 14 had a temporal lobectomy. For the next 11 years, she complained of occasional transient "butterflies in the stomach" and had already been driving in New Zealand for 6 years without any trouble. She had one of these feelings while being recorded on video; there was no hint of clouding of consciousness, her EEG remained undisturbed and it seemed reasonable to assume that they were merely expressions of anxiety in someone who was very aware of the possibility of a recurrence of her epilepsy.

Involuntary movements

Most would accept that tics and such rareties as paroxysmal choreo-athetosis are not epileptic, but difficulties do occur with myoclonus. On some occasions, myoclonic jerks are clearly not epileptic – such jerks when going off to sleep are an example – but they may also be part of the spectrum of epilepsy. In such a variable condition as this, each case has to be considered on its merits and a decision made accordingly.

Reflex epilepsy

On a number of occasions it has been suggested that reflex epilepsy in a particular patient in whom the attacks have always occurred in a stereotyped pattern should not be considered as a bar to driving. Pain, sexual activity, music, reading and the TV are some of the stimuli that have been cited. In none of the cases studied have there seemed adequate grounds for considering a relaxation of the regulations; fits may occur at other times, some of the triggers may operate while the patient is driving and the current rules of 2 years' freedom from attacks while awake would not seem unduly harsh.

Sleep

Drivers undoubtedly do fall asleep at the wheel and have accidents as a result, but such an explanation can, on the evidence presented, be highly unlikely. An HGV driver climbed into the cab of his lorry, drove straight into the back of a stationary vehicle some 25 yards ahead and was then found confused; a woman had just come out of a shop, within a few hundred yards had collided with another car and did not recover consciousness for 20 min despite there being no evidence that she had received a head injury. In neither of these two cases was the explanation of sleep, which had been put forward to explain both accidents, accepted.

Fits and faints

The distinction between fits and faints can be extremely difficult and a fit can be provoked by a faint. On the one hand, lack of awareness of a syndrome such as micturition syncope may lead to an erroneous diagnosis of epilepsy and on the other, a condition, which on the history alone may sound like syncope can turn out to be epilepsy. A woman complained of having fainted on several occasions over the years, each episode having occurred when blood was being taken from her. It was decided to check her haemoglobin and the specimen was taken with the patient lying down and using the sphygmomanometer cuff as a tourniquet. The patient had a major tonic/clonic convulsion within seconds of the introduction of the needle, she did not exhibit pallor and her blood pressure, taken within seconds of the onset of the fit, was mildly elevated.

The decision that a person should not be issued with a driving licence, or have it revoked, is one that should never be taken lightly and in each case all the available facts should be studied and weighed up. Some of the difficulties in arriving at a just decision have been illustrated and occasionally, when there are conflicting views and when the reliability of a witness is an issue, a Magistrate's court, where evidence may be taken on oath, is the best place for the case to be resolved.

Summary of Proceedings – Driving Licence Regulations at Home and Abroad

M. PARSONAGE

The David Lewis Centre for Epilepsy, Alderley Edge, Cheshire and formerly of the Neurology Department, General Infirmary, Leeds, UK

The purpose of the first part of this final chapter is to draw attention to some of the most important points made in the preceding chapters. The second part will be devoted to a brief commentary on the regulations for driving licence holders in relation to epilepsy in a number of countries throughout the world and to some recommendations made by an International Commission.

In his introductory chapter Dr Richard Godwin-Austen comments on the fact that, because the detailed application of driving licence regulations is often a matter of judgment and interpretation, patients may be given conflicting advice by doctors. He sets out the new regulations which have been in operation since April 1982, commenting on the lack of definition as regards "suffering from epilepsy", the doubtful risks in relation to sleep seizures, the assessment of risk in general to the public and the possibility of special consideration being given to certain cases of so-called reflex epilepsy and perhaps also to those individuals who only drive occasionally. In addition, he raises the question of the need for more specific regulations and the need for caution in view of the doctor's legal responsibilities in relation to any advice he may give.

In his chapter, Dr John Taylor points out the impossibility of determining what part medical factors, including epileptic seizures, play in serious road traffic accidents. In a series of 1300 less severe police-reported accidents he concludes that epilepsy caused at least half of them, whereas heart conditions and strokes caused only 18%. Furthermore, the notification rate of drivers of their pre-accident condition was found to be low and, predictably, the average age of collapse due to epilepsy was lower than in the heart and stroke cases. Finally, he reminds us that third party insurance cover does not operate in cases of collapse at the wheel and of the frequency of insulin-treated diabetes as a cause of epileptic seizures in addition to the other problems to which it may give rise.

In their chapter Drs Peter Harvey and Anthony Hopkins have confirmed from their recent research by questionnaire that there is considerable variation as regards advice given by neurophysicians in relation to epilepsy and driving; furthermore, it

Driving and Epilepsy – and Other Causes of Impaired Consciousness, edited by R. B. Godwin-Austen and M. L. E. Espir, 1983: Royal Society of Medicine International Congress and Symposium Series No. 60, published jointly by Academic Press Inc. (London) Ltd., and the Royal Society of Medicine.

would appear that this is due to misunderstandings about the regulations and to differences of opinion at clinical level. Their criticism of what they see as the lack of communication between the DVLC and its Medical Advisory Panel can surely be overcome by the simple expedient of making direct contact with the Medical Advisers to the Department of Transport in cases of doubt and probably not many would support their recommendation of compulsory reporting of epilepsy to licensing authorities.

The toxic effects of anti-epileptic drug therapy may affect those functions such as perception, reaction times, co-ordination, vigilance, etc., which are particularly necessary when driving. Dr Michael Trimble points out in his chapter that they may be affected by medical conditions and their treatment and so impair driving and he discusses the various tests which have been used to assess them. Clearly, patients should be warned of effects that might impair their driving, not forgetting that some anti-epileptic drugs are also used in the treatment of other conditions.

In addition to our pre-occupation about epilepsy and driving Dr David Parkes discusses not dissimilar hazards which may be caused by disorders of sleep. These are nowadays better understood and in his chapter he considers the common causes of daytime drowsiness such as a poor night's sleep, fatigue, alcohol and sedative drugs. Among the less common causes are narcolepsy, essential hypersomnolence and sleep apnoea; unfortunately however these constitute a "grey area" which does not permit of any firm general recommendations about fitness to drive and these can only be made on an individual basis.

In Dr Michael Espir's chapter are set out those issues that are clear and generally accepted. Thus, the types of vehicle concerned are defined in law and patients need to be told exactly what the law is with regard to their fitness to drive. In contrast, epilepsy itself is not defined in law and the doctor himself must make the diagnosis without legal obligation to report it. It must of course be distinguished from other conditions which may mimic it and for which there may be no specific legislation. If a primary cerebral cause for a single seizure is found then epilepsy must be diagnosed and the 2-year rule applies. If however there was an exceptional precipitating factor which is unlikely to recur then epilepsy should not be diagnosed. When treatment is withdrawn driving should cease but for how long is debatable.

To put matters into perspective, in his chapter, Dr Andrew Raffle, in discussing medical problems concerning HGV/PSV drivers, reminds us that illness is not an important factor in causing road traffic accidents. The possibility of concealment of epilepsy has to be borne in mind and Dr Raffle quotes five such instances in a total of 24 cases of epilepsy causing accidents at the wheel. Suspicion should be aroused if a driver goes to a doctor other than his own for completion of a medical certificate or is carrying tablets in his jacket pocket. Dr Raffle concludes by making it clear why there must be higher standards of qualification for HGV/PSV licence holders than those required for private drivers.

So-called professional drivers, such as chauffeurs and sales representatives, need special consideration, as Dr Felicity Edwards indicates in her chapter on this subject. Here the need to take medication under continuous medical supervision and to keep accurate medical records is paramount. She draws attention to the valuable role of Occupational Health Services in safeguarding the health of a workforce and also to the Employment Medical Advisory Service (EMAS) in assisting employers, employees and trade unions in relation to prevention of ill-health and to rehabilitation and re-training. She also reminds us that there are neither licence requirements nor fixed standards of medical fitness for drivers of powered vehicles (trucks, loaders, etc.) on factory or other sites, with the result that standards have not been laid down consistently throughout the country.

Professor Bryan Jennett in his chapter draws attention to the not yet widely recognized fact that craniotomy carries with it similar risks of causing epilepsy to those accruing from head injuries. There are high- and low-risk cases in both circumstances and data about the frequency of epilepsy after craniotomy are now becoming available. Professor Jennett stresses the importance of early epilepsy in increasing the risks of late epilepsy and his familiar chart of combinations of risk factors retains its usefulness. He also draws attention to the increased risk of post-operative epilepsy if there is a pre-operative history of epilepsy and it is noteworthy that British neurosurgeons are nowadays advising anti-epileptic medication in cases which carry a 20–40% risk of epilepsy.

Whatever regulations may be formulated there will always be problem cases requiring the exercise of good judgment. Dr Peter Gautier-Smith in describing his experience as a member of the Medical Advisory Panel to the Department of Transport has found that the majority of drivers accept revocation of their licences with good grace and that many manage remarkably well in spite of being unable to drive. Sometimes false testimony is given, especially when the motivation is strong, and the series of cases Dr Gautier-Smith recounts are illustrative of this and of other problems due to muddled thinking, ignorance of the law and difficulties related to different kinds of seizure. Epilepsy and syncope continue to be confused, thus leading to wrong conclusions and he rightly stresses that the decision to advise revocation of a driving licence should only be made after a careful consideration of all the available facts.

Driving Licence Regulations Abroad

Many developed countries have devised soundly based regulations for the issue of driving licences in relation to epilepsy, particularly in Western Europe and North America. Generally speaking, they have tended to be somewhat more flexible than those in force in this country, although the need for stricter regulations for HGV/PSV licence holders is universally recognized. Varying stress is laid on the importance of EEG findings and the concession for sleep seizures has not been widely practised. A 2-year period of freedom from seizures has been adopted almost universally and many countries stress the desirability of considering cases on their individual merits, notably the Scandinavian countries.

In March 1978 Epilepsy International (EI) set up a special Commission to enquire into the driving licence regulations adopted in various countries throughout the world and to make recommendations on a basis of a consensus of opinion. It was hoped that such recommendations might promote greater uniformity of regulations throughout the world and I would now like to refer briefly to the recommendations which were made after the completion of a wide-ranging enquiry.

With regard to definition, it was felt that seizures unassociated with impairment of awareness and/or loss of motor control need not be a bar to driving provided that medication is taken regularly under supervision. The recommended period of freedom from seizures should be 1–2 years but could be less on the recommendation of a specialist physician. The concession for sleep seizures has not however been recommended and the EEG findings are regarded as rarely likely to be decisive in the assessment of fitness to drive.

If there has been a recurrence of seizures for any reason following the prescribed period of freedom the EI Commission recommends that driving should cease for 6 months and not be resumed until thorough investigation has been carried out.

Driving need not be banned if seizures have occurred during febrile or acute cerebral or toxic illnesses. It was considered that an isolated seizure need not necessarily be a bar to drive provided that the risk of further seizures is considered low after careful assessment.

The EI Commission make reference to the role of the specialist physician as an assessor of medical fitness in persons with histories of epilepsy. Thus, it was felt that such a specialist should have a recognized special interest and expertise in the field of epilepsy. Furthermore, in the assessment of any case the reliability of the individual with regard to driving record, degree of compliance and general behaviour are considered to be much more important than the minutiae of the epilepsy. Mandatory reporting of epilepsy to licensing authorities is regarded as generally unacceptable, even though it is still practised in some countries. The Commission conceded however that there might be special circumstances in which it might be proper to report cases, as, for example, when there is unsatisfactory compliance as regards taking medication or when associated psychiatric disorder might make driving a danger to the public. Authorities in some countries would also regard non-compliance in regard to medical examinations as a bar to holding a driving licence.

The EI Commission favours the idea of compulsory medical reviews, preferably undertaken by an independent physician. It has also emphasized the importance of drivers with controlled epilepsy giving an undertaking to adhere to instructions as regards taking their drugs, to carry out any general advice they may be given and to report any circumstances which might impair their fitness to drive. In these circumstances drivers are advised to stop driving immediately, seek medical advice and not resume driving until it is considered safe for them to do so.

The EI Commission has endorsed the widespread acknowledgment of the necessity for much stricter regulations with regard to the granting of licences to drive public service and heavy goods vehicles. The present requirement in this country of freedom from seizures since the age of 5 years has been regarded by the EI Commission as somewhat too rigid and it is felt that greater equity might be served by assessing each case individually. Thus, the likelihood of a recurrence following seizures in childhood may often be very low and the same would probably apply to an individual who has had no seizures for 10 years if none had occurred since he reached the age of 20 years.

The availability of special appeal panels is recommended. This would enable individuals to challenge unfavourable decisions which they consider unjustified and they are invaluable in cases of special medical difficulty giving rise to differences of opinion.

In general terms the EI Commission emphasized the importance of assessment of cases individually and recommended that the granting of licences should be sufficiently permissive to be consistent with acceptable risks with regard to road safety. This should tend to reduce the incidence of concealment and encourage compliance. Particular stress is laid on the importance of personal responsibility and behaviour, especially with regard to the consumption of alcohol. Finally, the Commission recommended that temporary licences might be granted in exceptional cases, with perhaps waiving of the prescribed period of freedom from seizures, while longer periods of freedom could be required if there was an unusually high risk of relapse.

Reference

International Summary of Driving Licence Regulations. Epilepsy International. January 1982. Via G. Gozzi 1, 20129 Milano, Italy.